# THE "F" WORDS

*Ulrica Z. Wing Leigh*

*Reform Publisher*

Flee **<u>FORNICATION</u>**.
Every sin that a man doeth is
w-i-t-h-o-u-t the body;
*but*
he that committeth
**<u>FORNICATION</u>**
sinneth against  (w-i-t-h-i-n) his
own body.


**W-H-A-T?**


know ye *not* that your body is the
temple of the Holy Ghost which is
in you, which ye have of God,
*and*
**<u>YE</u> <u>ARE</u> <u>NOT</u> <u>YOUR</u> <u>OWN</u>?**
For ye are bought with a price:
*therefore* GLORIFY GOD IN
YOUR B-O-D-Y, *and*
IN YOUR S-P-I-R-I-T, WHICH
ARE GOD'S.
(1 Corinthians 6:18-20)

# TABLE OF CONTENTS

# PHYSICAL

## OLD TESTAMENT

Thou shalt not commit **ADULTERY.** (Exodus 20:14)

Do not prostitute thy daughter, to cause her to be a **WHORE;** lest the land fall to **WHOREDOM,** and the land become full of wickedness. (Leviticus 19:29)

And the man that committeth **ADULTERY** with another man's wife, even he that committeth **ADULTERY** with his neighbour's wife, the **ADULTERER** and the **ADULTERESS** shall surely be put to death. (Leviticus 20:10)

They shall not take a wife that is a **WHORE,** or profane; neither shall they take a woman put away from her husband: for he is holy unto his God. Thou shalt sanctify him therefore; for he offereth the bread of thy God: he shall be holy unto thee: for I the LORD, which sanctify you, am holy. And the daughter of any priest, if she profane herself by playing the **WHORE,** she profaneth her father: she shall be burnt with fire. And he that is the HIGH PRIEST among his brethren, upon whose head the anointing oil was poured, and that is consecrated to put on the garments, shall not uncover his head, nor rend his clothes; Neither shall he go in to any dead body, nor defile himself for his father, or for his mother; Neither shall he go out of the sanctuary, nor profane the sanctuary of his God; for THE CROWN OF THE ANOINTING OIL OF HIS GOD IS UPON HIM: I am the LORD. And he shall take a wife in her VIRGINITY. A WIDOW, or a DIVORCED WOMAN, or PROFANE, or AN **HARLOT,** these shall he *not* take: but he shall take a VIRGIN OF HIS OWN PEOPLE to wife. NEITHER SHALL HE PROFANE HIS SEED AMONG HIS PEOPLE: for I the LORD do sanctify him. (Leviticus 21:7-15)

Neither shalt thou commit **ADULTERY.** (Deuteronomy 5:18)

Then they shall bring out the damsel to the door of her father's house, and the men of her city shall STONE HER WITH STONES THAT SHE DIE: because she hath wrought folly in Israel, to play the **WHORE** in her father's house: so shalt thou put evil away from among you. (Deuteronomy 22:21)

There shall be no **WHORE** of the daughters of Israel, *nor* a SODOMITE of the sons of Israel. Thou shalt not bring the hire of a **WHORE**, or the price of a dog (male sacred prostitute), into the house of the Lord thy God for any vow: for even BOTH THESE ARE A-B-O-M-I-N-A-T-I-O-N unto the Lord thy God. (Deuteronomy 23:17-18)

The eye also of the **ADULTERER** waiteth for the twilight, saying, No eye shall see me: and disguiseth his face. (Job 24:15)

But unto the WICKED God saith, What hast thou to do to declare my statutes, or that thou shouldest take

6

my covenant in thy mouth? Seeing THOU H-A-T-E-S-T INSTRUCTION, and CASTETH MY WORDS BEHIND THEE. When thou sawest a THIEF, then thou consentedst with him, and hast been partaker with **ADULTERERS.** Thou givest thy MOUTH TO EVIL, and THY TONGUE FRAMETH DECEIT. Thou SITTEST and SPEAKEST AGAINST THY BROTHER; thou SLANDEREST own mother's son. These things hast thou done, and **I kept silence;** <u>thou thoughtest that I was altogether such an one as thyself</u>: *but* I WILL REPROVE THEE, and set them in order before thine eyes.

# NOW CONSIDER THIS,

# YE THAT FORGET GOD,

# LEST I TEAR YOU IN PIECES,

# *and* THERE BE NONE TO DELIVER.

(Psalm 50:16-22)

But whoso committeth **ADULTERY** with a woman lacketh understanding: he that doeth it destroyeth his own soul. (Proverbs 6:32)

For a **WHORE** is a deep ditch; and a strange woman is a narrow pit. (Proverbs 23:27)

Whoso loveth wisdom rejoiceth his father: *but* he that keepeth company with **HARLOTS** spendeth his substance. (Proverbs 29:3)

Such is the way of an **ADULTEROUS** woman; she eateth, and wipeth her mouth, and saith, I HAVE DONE NO WICKEDNESS. (Proverbs 30:20)

Hear ye therefore the word of the LORD, all ye of the captivity, whom I have sent from Jerusalem to Babylon: Thus saith the LORD of hosts, the God of Israel, of Ahab the son of Kolaiah, and of Zedekiah the son of Maaseiah, WHICH PROPHESY A LIE UNTO YOU IN M-Y NAME; Behold, I will deliver them *into* the hand of Nebuchadrezzar king of Babylon; and he shall slay them before your eyes; And of them shall be taken up a curse by all the captivity of Judah which are in Babylon, saying, **The LORD make thee like Zedekiah and like Ahab, whom the king of Babylon *roasted* in the fire;** *Because* THEY HAVE COMMITTED V-I-L-L-A-N-Y IN ISRAEL, and HAVE COMMITTED **ADULTERY** WITH THEIR NEIGHOUR'S WIVES, and HAVE SPOKEN LYING WORDS IN MY NAME, which I have *not* commanded them; even I know, and am a witness, saith the LORD. (Jeremiah 29:20-23)

The beginning of the word of the LORD by Hosea. And the LORD said to Hosea, Go, take unto thee a WIFE OF **WHOREDOMS** and CHILDREN OF **WHOREDOMS:** for the land hath committed great

8

WHOREDOM, D-E-P-A-R-T-I-N-G    F-R-O-M
T-H-E    L-O-R-D. (Hosea 1:2)

Then said the LORD unto me, Go yet, love a woman
beloved of her friend, yet an **ADULTERESS,
according to the love of the LORD toward the
children of Israel, who look to other gods, and
love flagons of wine.**  So I bought her to me for
fifteen pieces of silver, and for an homer of barley,
and an half homer of barley:  And I said unto her,
Thou shalt abide for me many days; THOU SHALT
N-O-T PLAY THE **HARLOT,** and thou shalt not
be for another man: so will I also be for thee.  For
the children of Israel shall abide many days without
a king, and without a prince, and without a sacrifice,
and without an image, and without an ephod, and
without teraphim:  *Afterward* SHALL THE
CHILDREN OF ISRAEL RETURN, and SEEK
THE LORD THEIR GOD, and DAVID THEIR
KING; and SHALL FEAR THE LORD and HIS
GOODNESS IN THE LATTER DAYS. (Hosea
3:1-5)

And the LORD took me as I followed the flock, and
the LORD said unto me, Go, prophesy unto my
people Israel.  Now therefore hear thou the word of
the LORD: Thou sayest, Prophesy not against Israel,
and drop not thy word against the house of Isaac.
*Therefore* thus saith the LORD; THY WIFE SHALL
BE AN **HARLOT** IN THE CITY, and THY SONS
and THY DAUGHTERS SHALL FALL BY THE
SWORD, and THY LAND SHALL BE DIVIDED
BY LINE, and THOU SHALT DIE IN A
POLLUTED LAND: and Israel shall surely go into
captivity forth of his land. (Amos 7:15-17)

# PHYSICAL

## NEW TESTAMENT

Ye have heard that it was said by them of old time, THOU SHALT NOT COMMIT **ADULTERY:** *But* I say unto you, THAT WHOSOEVER LOOKETH ON A WOMAN TO LUST AFTER HER HATH COMMITTED **ADULTERY** WITH HER ALREADY IN HIS HEART. And if thy *right eye* offend thee, PLUCK IT OUT, and cast it from thee: for IT IS PROFITABLE FOR THEE THAT ONE OF THY MEMBERS SHOULD PERISH, and NOT THAT THY WHOLE BODY SHOULD BE CAST INTO H-E-L-L. And if thy *right hand* offend thee, CUT IT OFF, and cast it from thee: for IT IS PROFITABLE FOR THEE THAT ONE OF THY MEMBERS SHOULD PERISH, and NOT THAT THY WHOLE BODY SHOULD BE CAST INTO H-E-L-L. It hath been said, Whosoever shall put away his wife, let him give her a writing of divorcement: But I say unto you, That whosoever shall put away his wife, saving for the cause of **FORNICATION,** causeth her to commit **ADULTERY:** and whosoever shall marry her that is divorced committeth **ADULTERY.** (Matthew 5:27-32)

And Jesus said, Are ye also yet without understanding? Do not ye yet understand, that whatsoever entereth in at the mouth goeth into the belly, and is cast out into the draught? *But* THOSE THINGS WHICH PROCEED OUT OF THE

MOUTH COME FORTH FROM THE HEART; and THEY DEFILE THE MAN. FOR OUT OF THE HEART PROCEED <u>EVIL THOUGHTS</u>, <u>MURDERS</u>, **ADULTERIES, FORNICATIONS,** <u>THEFTS</u>, <u>FALSE WITNESS</u>, <u>BLASPHEMIES</u>: THESE ARE THE THINGS WHICH DEFILE A MAN: but to eat with unwashen hands defileth *not* a man. (Matthew 15:16-20)

The Pharisees also came unto him, <u>tempting</u> him, and saying unto him, (Q:) Is it lawful for a man to put away his wife for every cause? And he answered and said unto them, (A:) Have ye not read, that he which made them at the beginning made them MALE and FEMALE, And said, For this cause shall a man leave father and mother, and shall cleave to his wife: and they twain shall be one flesh? Wherefore they are no more twain, but one flesh. What therefore God hath joined together, let not man put asunder. They say unto him, (Q:) Why did Moses then command to give a writing of divorcement, and to put her away? He saith unto them, (A:) Moses BECAUSE OF THE HARDNESS OF YOUR HEARTS suffered you to put away your wives: *but* from the beginning it was not so. And I say unto you, Whosoever shall put away his wife, except it be for **FORNICATION (ANY SEXUAL ACTIVITY OUTSIDE OF A MALE/FEMALE MARRIAGE COVENANT),** and shall marry another, committeth **ADULTERY:** and whoso marrieth her which is put away doth commit **ADULTERY.** His disciples say unto him, If the case of the man be so with his wife, it is not good to marry. But he said unto them, All men cannot receive this saying, save they to whom it is given. For there are some eunuchs, which were so born from their mother's womb: and there are some eunuchs, which were made eunuchs of men: and there be eunuchs, which have made themselves eunuchs for the kingdom of heaven's sake. He that is able to receive it, let him receive it. Then were there brought unto him little children, that he should put his hands on them, and pray: and the disciples rebuked them. But Jesus said, *Suffer little children, and forbid them not, to come unto me: for of such is the kingdom of heaven.* And he laid his hands on them, and departed thence. And, behold, one came and said unto him, (Q:) Good Master, what good thing shall I do, that I may have eternal life? And he said unto him, Why callest thou me good? there is none good but one, that is, God: but if thou wilt enter into life, (A:) K-E-E-P  T-HE  C-O-M-M-A-N-D-M-E-N-T-S. He saith unto him, *Which?* Jesus said, THOU SHALT DO NO MURDER, THOU SHALT NOT COMMIT **ADULTERY,** THOU SHALT NOT STEAL, THOU SHALT NOT BEAR FALSE WITNESS, HONOUR THY FATHER AND THY MOTHER: *and,* THOU SHALT LOVE THY NEIGHBOUR AS THYSELF. (Matthew 19:3-19)

But what think ye? A certain man had two sons; and he came to the FIRST, and said, Son, go work to day in my vineyard. He answered and said, **I will not:** *but* AFTERWARD HE REPENTED, and WENT. And he came to the SECOND, and said likewise. And he answered and said, **I go, sir:** *and* WENT N-O-T. (Q:) Whether of them twain did the will of his father? They say unto him, (A:) *The first.* Jesus saith unto them, Verily I say unto you, That THE PUBLICANS and THE **HARLOTS** GO INTO THE KINGDOM OF GOD BEFORE YOU.

For John came unto you in the way of righteousness, and YE BELIEVED HIM NOT: *b-u-t* THE PUBLICANS and THE **HARLOTS** BELIEVED HIM: and ye, when ye had seen it, REPENTED N-O-T afterward, that ye might believe him. (Matthew 21:28-32)

And he saith unto them, Are ye so without understanding also? Do ye not perceive, that whatsoever thing from without entereth into the man, it cannot defile him; Because it entereth not into his heart, but into the belly, and goeth out into the draught, purging all meats? And he said, THAT WHICH COMETH O-U-T OF THE MAN, THAT DEFILETH THE MAN. FOR FROM WITHIN, OUT OF THE H-E-A-R-T OF MEN, PROCEED EVIL THOUGHTS, **ADULTERIES, FORNICATIONS,** MURDERS, THEFTS, COVETOUSNESS, WICKEDNESS, DECEIT, LASCIVIOUSNESS, AN EVIL EYE, BLASPHEMY, PRIDE, FOOLISHNESS: All these evil things come from W-I-T-H-I-N, and defile the man. (Mark 7:18-23)

And the Pharisees came to him, and asked him, (Q:) Is it lawful for a man to put away his wife? tempting him. And he answered and said unto them, What did Moses command you? And they said, Moses suffered to write a bill of divorcement, and to put her away. And Jesus answered and said unto them, (A:) FOR THE H-A-R-D-N-E-S-S O-F Y-O-U-R H-E-A-R-T he wrote you this precept. But from the beginning of the creation God made them MALE and FEMALE. For this cause shall a man leave his father and mother, and cleave to his wife; And they twain shall be one flesh: so then

14

they are no more twain, but one flesh. What therefore God hath joined together, let not man put asunder. And in the house his disciples asked him again of the same matter. And he saith unto them, Whosoever shall put away his wife, and marry another, committeth **ADULTERY** against her. And if a woman shall put away her husband, and be married to another, she committeth **ADULTERY**. And they brought young children to him, that he should touch them: and his disciples rebuked those that brought them. But when Jesus saw it, he was much displeased, and said unto them, *Suffer the little children to come unto me, and forbid them not: for of such is the kingdom of God.* Verily I say unto you, **Whosoever shall not receive the kingdom of God as a little child, he shall not enter therein.** And he took them up in his arms, put his hands upon them, and blessed them. And when he was gone forth into the way, there came one running, and kneeled to him, and asked him, (Q:) Good Master, what shall I do that I may inherit eternal life? And Jesus said unto him, Why callest thou me good? there is none good but one, that is, God. (A:) THOU KNOWEST THE C-O-M-M-A-N-D-M-E-N-T-S, DO NOT COMMIT **ADULTERY,** DO NOT KILL, DO NOT STEAL, DO NOT BEAR FALSE WITNESS, DEFRAUD NOT, HONOUR THY FATHER AND MOTHER. (Mark 10:2-19)

And he said, A CERTAIN MAN HAD TWO SONS: And the younger of them said to his father, **Father, give me the portion of goods that falleth to me. And he divided unto them his living.** And not many days after the younger son gathered all together, and took his journey into a FAR COUNTRY, and there WASTED his substance

15

with riotous living. And when he had spent all, there arose a mighty famine in that land; and he began to be in want. And he went and joined himself to a citizen of that country; and he sent him into his fields to feed SWINE. And he would fain have filled his belly with the husks that the swine did eat: and no man gave unto him. And WHEN HE CAME TO HIMSELF, he said, How many hired servants of my father's have bread enough and to spare, and I perish with hunger! I will arise and go to my father, and will say unto him, FATHER, I HAVE SINNED AGAINST HEAVEN, and BEFORE THEE, and AM NO MORE WORTHY TO BE CALLED THY SON: MAKE ME AS ONE OF THY HIRED SERVANTS. And he arose, and came to his father. *But* when he was yet a great way off, his father saw him, and had COMPASSION, and ran, and fell on his neck, and kissed him. And the son said unto him, FATHER, I HAVE SINNED AGAINST HEAVEN, and IN THY SIGHT, and AM NO MORE WORTHY TO BE CALLED THY SON. *But* the father said to his servants, Bring forth the *best* robe, and put it on him; and put a ring on his hand, and shoes on his feet: And bring hither the fatted calf, and kill it; and let us eat, and be merry: FOR THIS MY SON WAS DEAD, and IS ALIVE AGAIN; HE WAS LOST, and IS FOUND. And they began to be merry. Now his elder son was in the field: and as he came and drew nigh to the house, he heard musick and dancing. And he called one of the servants, and asked what these things meant. And he said unto him, Thy brother is come; and thy father hath killed the fatted calf, because he hath received him safe and sound. And he was angry, and would not go in: therefore came his father out, and intreated him. And he answering said to his father, Lo, these many years do "I" serve thee, neither transgressed I at any time thy commandment: and yet thou never gavest "ME" a kid, that I might make merry with my friends:  But as soon as this thy son was come, which hath devoured thy living with **HARLOTS,** thou hast killed for him the fatted calf.  And he said unto him, Son, thou art ever with me, and ALL THAT I HAVE IS THINE.  It was meet that we should make merry, and be glad: *for* THIS THY BROTHER WAS DEAD, and IS ALIVE AGAIN; and WAS LOST, and IS FOUND. (Luke 15:11-32)

And he said unto them, **Ye are they which justify yourselves before men;** *but* G-O-D  K-N-O-W-E-T-H  Y-O-U-R  H-E-A-R-T-S: for that which is highly esteemed among men is A-B-O-M-I-N-A-T-I-O-N in the sight of God.  The law and the prophets were until John: since that time the kingdom of God is preached, and EVERY MAN PRESSETH INTO IT.  *And* IT IS EASIER FOR HEAVEN and EARTH TO PASS, THAN ONE TITTLE OF THE LAW TO FAIL.  Whosoever putteth away his wife, and marrieth another, committeth **ADULTERY:** and whosoever marrieth her that is put away from her husband committeth **ADULTERY.**  (Luke 16:15-18)

And he spake this parable unto certain which **trusted in themselves that they were righteous, and despised others:**  Two men went up into the temple to pray; the one a <u>PHARISEE</u>, and the other a <u>PUBLICAN</u>.  The <u>PHARISEE</u> stood and prayed thus with himself, <u>God, I THANK THEE, THAT I AM NOT AS OTHER MEN ARE,</u> extortioners, <u>unjust, **ADULTERER,**</u> or even as this publican.  I fast twice in the week, I give tithes of all that I possess. And the PUBLICAN, STANDING AFAR OFF, WOULD NOT LIFT UP SO MUCH AS HIS EYES UNTO HEAVEN, but SMOTE UPON HIS BREAST, SAYING, GOD BE MERCIFUL TO ME A SINNER. *I tell you, t-h-i-s man went down to his house justified rather than the other:* **for every one that EXALTETH himself shall be ABASED;** *and he that HUMBLETH himself shall be EXALTED.* And they brought unto him also infants, that he would touch them: but when his disciples saw it, they rebuked them. But Jesus called them unto him, and said, *Suffer little children to come unto me, and forbid them not: for of such is the kingdom of God.* Verily I say unto you, Whosoever shall not receive the kingdom of God as a little child shall in no wise enter therein. And a certain ruler asked him, saying, (A:) Good Master, what shall I do to inherit eternal life? And Jesus said unto him, Why callest thou me good? none is good, save one, that is, God. (A:) THOU KNOWEST THE C-O-M-M-A-N-D-M-E-N-T-S, DO NOT COMMIT **ADULTERY,** DO NOT KILL, DO NOT STEAL, DO NOT BEAR FALSE WITNESS, HONOUR THY FATHER AND THY MOTHER. (Luke 18:9-10)

And early in the morning he came again into the temple, and all the people came unto him; and he sat down, and taught them. And the scribes and Pharisees brought unto him a woman taken in **ADULTERY;** and when they had set her in the midst, They say unto him, MASTER, THIS WOMAN WAS TAKEN IN **ADULTERY,** IN THE VERY ACT. Now Moses in the law commanded us, that such should be stoned: but what sayest thou? This they said, tempting him, that they might have to accuse him. But Jesus stooped down, and with his finger wrote on the ground, as though he heard them not. So when they continued asking him, he lifted up himself, and said unto them, HE THAT IS WITHOUT SIN AMONG YOU, LET HIM FIRST CAST A STONE AT HER. And again he stooped down, and wrote on the ground. And they which heard it, being *convicted by their own conscience,* went out one by one, beginning at the eldest, even unto the last: and Jesus was left alone, and the woman standing in the midst. When Jesus had lifted up himself, and saw none but the woman, he said unto her, Woman, where are those thine accusers? hath no man condemned thee? She said, No man, Lord. And Jesus said unto her, *Neither do I condemn thee:* GO, *and* S-I-N N-O M-O-R-E. (John 8:2-11)

Wherefore my sentence is, that we trouble not them, which from among the Gentiles are turned to God: But that we write unto them, that they ABSTAIN FROM POLLUTIONS OF IDOLS, and FROM **FORNICATION,** and FROM THINGS STRANGLED, and FROM BLOOD. For Moses of old time hath in every city them that preach him, being read in the synagogues every sabbath day. Then pleased it the apostles and elders with the whole church, to send chosen men of their own company to Antioch with Paul and Barnabas; namely, Judas surnamed Barsabas and Silas, chief men among the brethren: And they wrote letters by them after this manner; The apostles and elders and brethren send greeting unto the brethren which are of the Gentiles in Antioch and Syria and Cilicia. Forasmuch as we have heard, that certain which went out from us have troubled you with words, subverting your souls, saying, Ye must be circumcised, and keep the law: to whom we gave *no* such commandment: It seemed good unto us, being assembled with one accord, to send chosen men unto you with our beloved Barnabas and Paul, <u>Men that have hazarded their lives for the name of our Lord Jesus Christ</u>. We have sent therefore Judas and Silas, who shall also tell you the same things by mouth. For it seemed good to the Holy Ghost, and to us, to lay upon you no greater burden than these **necessary things;** <u>THAT YE ABSTAIN FROM MEATS OFFERED TO IDOLS</u>, and <u>FROM BLOOD</u>, and <u>FROM THINGS STRANGLED</u>, and <u>FROM **FORNICATION**</u>: from which *if* ye keep yourselves, *ye shall do well.* Fare ye well. (Acts 1519-29)

As touching the <u>Gentiles which believe</u>, we have written and concluded that they observe no such thing, save only that they <u>KEEP THEMSELVES FROM THINGS OFFERED TO IDOLS</u>, and <u>FROM BLOOD</u>, and <u>FROM STANGLED</u>, and <u>FROM **FORNICATION**</u>. (Acts 21:25)

**For the WRATH OF GOD is revealed from heaven against *all* ungodliness and unrighteousness of men, who hold the truth in unrighteousness;** Because that which may be known of God is manifest in them; for God hath shewed it unto them. For the invisible things of him from the creation of the world are clearly seen, being understood by the things that are made, even his eternal power and Godhead; S-O T-H-A-T T-H-E-Y A-R-E W-I-T-H-O-U-T E-X-C-U-S-E: Because that, when they knew God, they glorified him not as God, *neither* were <u>thankful</u>; *but*

20

BECAME VAIN IN THEIR IMAGINATIONS, and THEIR FOOLISH HEART WAS DARKENED. Professing themselves to be wise, THEY BECAME F-O-O-L-S, And changed the glory of the uncorruptible God into an image made like to corruptible man, and to birds, and fourfooted beasts, and creeping things. Wherefore GOD ALSO GAVE THEM UP to uncleanness through THE LUSTS OF THEIR OWN HEARTS, TO DISHONOUR THEIR OWN BODIES BETWEEN THEMSELVES: **Who changed the truth of God into a l-i-e,** and worshipped and served the creature more than the Creator, who is blessed for ever. Amen. FOR THIS CAUSE GOD GAVE THEM UP UNTO V-I-L-E AFFECTIONS: FOR EVEN THEIR WOMEN DID CHANGE THE NATURAL USE INTO THAT WHICH IS A-G-A-I-N-S-T NATURE: AND LIKEWISE ALSO THE MEN, LEAVING THE NATURAL USE OF THE WOMAN, BURNED IN THEIR LUST ONE TOWARD ANOTHER; MEN WITH MEN WORKING THAT WHICH IS UNSEEMLY, and RECEIVING IN THEMSELVES THAT R-E-C-O-M-P-E-N-C-E OF THEIR ERROR WHICH WAS MEET. **And even as they did not like to retain God in their knowledge, God gave them over to a r-e-p-r-o-b-a-t-e m-i-n-d, to do those things which are not convenient;** BEING FILLED WITH A-L-L UNRIGHTEOUSNESS, **FORNICATION,** WICKEDNESS, COVETOUSNESS, MALICIOUSNESS, FULL OF ENVY, MURDER, DEBATE, DECEIT, MALIGNITY; WHISPERERS, BACKBITERS, HATERS OF GOD, DESPITEFUL, PROUD, BOASTERS, INVENTORS OF EVIL THINGS, DISOBEDIENT TO PARENTS, WITHOUT

UNDERSTANDING, COVENANTBREAKERS, WITHOUT NATURAL AFFECTION, IMPLACABLE, UNMERCIFUL: WHO KNOWING THE JUDGMENT OF GOD, THAT THEY WHICH COMMIT SUCH THINGS ARE WORTHY OF D-E-A-T-H, NOT ONLY DO THE SAME, *but* HAVE P-L-E-A-S-U-R-E IN THEM THAT DO THEM. (Romans 1:18-32)

Thou therefore which teachest *another*, teachest thou not THYSELF? thou that preachest A MAN SHOULD NOT STEAL, dost *thou* STEAL? Thou that sayest A MAN SHOULD NOT COMMIT **ADULTERY,** dost *thou* commit **ADULTERY?** thou that ABHORREST IDOLS, dost *thou* commit SACRILEGE? Thou that makest thy boast of the law, through breaking the law dishonourest thou God? **For the name of God is *blasphemed* among the Gentiles (ungodly) through you,** as it is written. (Romans 2:21-24)

Owe no man any thing, but to *love* one another: *for* HE THAT LOVETH ANOTHER HATH FULFILLED THE LAW. For this, Thou shalt not commit **ADULTERY,** Thou shalt not KILL, Thou shalt not STEAL, Thou shalt not bear FALSE WITNESS, Thou shalt not COVET; and if there be any other commandment, it is briefly comprehended in this saying, namely, THOU SHALT LOVE THY NEIGHBOUR AS THYSELF. Love worketh *no* ill to his neighbour: *therefore love i-s the fulfilling of the law.* And that, knowing the time, that NOW IT IS HIGH TIME TO AWAKE OUT OF SLEEP: for now is our salvation nearer than when we believed. The night is far spent, the day is at hand: let us therefore CAST OFF THE WORKS OF

DARKNESS, and let us put on the armour of light. Let us WALK HONESTLY, as in the day; *not* in rioting and drunkenness, not in chambering and wantonness, not in strife and envying. But PUT YE ON the Lord Jesus Christ, and MAKE N-O-T PROVISION FOR THE FLESH, TO FULFIL THE LUSTS THEREOF. (Romans 13:8-14)

It is reported commonly that there is **FORNICATION** among you, and such **FORNICATION** as is not so much as named among the Gentiles, that one should have his father's wife. And ye are puffed up, and have not rather mourned, that HE THAT HATH DONE THIS DEED MIGHT BE TAKEN AWAY FROM AMONG YOU. For I verily, as absent in body, but present in spirit, have **judged** already, as though I were present, concerning him that hath so done this deed, In the name of our Lord Jesus Christ, when ye are gathered together, and my spirit, with the power of our Lord Jesus Christ,

# TO DELIVER SUCH AN ONE UNTO

# S-A-T-A-N

# FOR THE DESTRUCTION OF THE

# F-L-E-S-H,

# THAT THE S-P-I-R-I-T MAY BE SAVED IN THE DAY OF THE LORD JESUS.

Your glorying is not good. Know ye not that a little leaven leaveneth the whole lump?  Purge out therefore the old leaven, that ye may be a new lump, as ye are unleavened. For even Christ our passover is sacrificed for us  Therefore let us keep the feast, not with old leaven, neither with the leaven of malice and wickedness; but with the unleavened bread of sincerity and truth.

## I wrote unto you in an epistle *n-o-t* to company with <u>FORNICATORS</u>:

## Yet not altogether with the <u>FORNICATORS</u> of this *world*, or with the <u>covetous</u>, or <u>extortioners</u>, or with <u>idolaters</u>; for then must ye needs go out of the world.

## B-u-t

now I have written unto you not to keep company, if any man that is called a *brother* ("brother" in Christ) be a **FORNICATOR**, or <u>covetous</u>, or an <u>idolator</u>, or a <u>railer</u>, or a <u>drunkard</u>, or an <u>extortioner</u>; **WITH SUCH AN ONE NO NOT TO EAT.** For what have I to do to judge them also that are

<u>w-i-t-h-o-u-t</u>?

do not ye judge them that are <u>W-I-T-H-I-N</u>?

*But* them that are

<u>w-i-t-h-o-u-t</u> God judgeth.

# Therefore PUT AWAY from among *yourselves* that wicked person.

(1 Corinthians 5:1-13)

**(Q:) Know ye not that the unrighteous shall not inherit the kingdom of God? (A:) Be not deceived:** neither **FORNICATORS,** nor IDOLATERS, nor ADULTERERS, nor EFFEMINATE, nor ABUSERS OF THEMSELVES WITH MANKIND, nor THIEVES, nor COVETOUS, nor DRUNKARDS, nor REVILERS, nor EXTORTIONERS, shall inherit the kingdom of God. And such *were* some of you: but ye are washed, but ye are sanctified, but ye are justified in the name of the Lord Jesus, and by the Spirit of our God. All things are lawful unto me, but ALL THINGS ARE N-O-T EXPEDIENT: all things are lawful for me, but I WILL N-O-T BE BROUGHT UNDER THE POWER OF ANY. Meats for the belly, and the belly for meats: but God shall **destroy** both it and them. Now THE BODY IS N-O-T FOR **FORNICATION,** but for the Lord; and the Lord for the body. And God hath both raised up the Lord, and will also raise up us by his own power. KNOW YE NOT THAT YOUR BODIES ARE THE MEMBERS OF CHRIST? shall I then take the members of Christ, and make them the members of an **HARLOT?** GOD FORBID. What? know ye not that he which is joined to an **HARLOT** is one body? for two, saith he, shall be one flesh. But he that is joined unto the

Lord is one spirit. FLEE **FORNICATION.** Every sin that a man doeth is without the body; but HE THAT COMMITTETH **FORNICATION** SINNETH AGAINST HIS OWN BODY. What? know ye not that your body is the temple of the Holy Ghost which is in you, which ye have of God, and **y-e a-r-e n-o-t y-o-u-r o-w-n? For ye are bought with a (high) price:** *therefore* GLORIFY GOD IN YOUR BODY, and IN YOUR SPIRIT, WHICH ARE GOD'S. (1 Corinthians 6:9-20)

Now concerning the things whereof ye wrote unto me: It is good for a man not to touch a woman. Nevertheless, TO AVOID **FORNICATION,** let every man have his own wife, and let every woman have her own husband. (1 Corinthians 7:1-2)

Moreover, brethren, I would not that ye should be ignorant, how that all our fathers were under the cloud, and all passed through the sea; And were all baptized unto Moses in the cloud and in the sea; And did all eat the same spiritual meat; And did all drink the same spiritual drink: for they drank of that spiritual Rock that followed them: and that Rock was Christ. ***But* with many of them God was not well pleased: for they were OVERTHROWN in the wilderness.** Now these things were our EXAMPLES, to the intent WE SHOULD N-O-T LUST AFTER EVIL THINGS, as they also lusted. *Neither* be ye IDOLATERS, as were some of them; as it is written, The people sat down to eat and drink, and rose up to play. NEITHER LET US COMMIT **FORNICATION,** as some of them committed, and **fell** in one day three and twenty thousand. *Neither* let is TEMPT CHRIST, as some of them also tempted, and were **destroyed of**

**serpents**.  *Neither* MURMER ye, as some of them also murmured, and were **destroyed of the destroyer.**  Now all these things happened unto them for EXAMPLES: and they are written for our ADMONITION, upon whom the ends of the world are come.  Wherefore let him that thinketh he standeth TAKE HEED lest he fall.  There hath no temptation taken you but such as is common to man: *b-u-t God is faithful, who will not suffer you to be tempted above that ye are able; but will with the temptation also make a way to escape, that ye may be able to bear it.*  Wherefore, my dearly beloved, FLEE FROM IDOLATRY.  (1 Corinthians 10:1-14)

For I fear, lest, when I come, I shall *not* find YOU such as "I" would, and that "I" shall be found unto YOU such as ye would *not*: lest there be DEBATES, ENVYINGS, WRATHS, STRIFES, BACKBITINGS, WHISPERINGS, SWELLINGS, TUMULTS: And lest, when I come again, my God will humble me among you, and that I shall bewail many which have sinned already, and HAVE N-O-T REPENTED OF THE UNCLEANNESS and **FORNICATION** and LASCIVIOUSNESS WHICH THEY HAVE COMMITTED.  (2 Corinthians 12:20-21)

Now the WORKS OF THE F-L-E-S-H are manifest, which are these; **ADULTERY, FORNICATION,** UNCLEANNESS, LASCIVIOUSNESS, IDOLATRY, WITCHCRAFT, HATRED, VARIANCE, EMULATIONS, WRATH, STRIFE, SEDITIONS, HERESIES, ENVYINGS, MURDERS, DRUNKENNESS, REVELLINGS, and THE

SUCH LIKE: of the which I tell you before, as I have also told you in time past, that (............)

# THEY WHICH DO SUCH THINGS SHALL N-O-T INHERIT THE KINGDOM OF GOD.

*But the FRUIT OF THE SPIRIT is <u>love</u>, <u>joy</u>, <u>peace</u>, <u>longsuffering</u>, <u>gentleness</u>, <u>goodness</u>, <u>faith</u>, <u>Meekness</u>, <u>temperance</u>: against such there is no law.* And they that are Christ's have (...............................)

# C-R-U-C-I-F-I-E-D

# THE FLESH WITH THE AFFECTIONS and LUSTS.

*If* we live in the Spirit, let us also walk in the Spirit. Let us N-O-T be desirous of VAIN GLORY, PROVOKING one another, ENVYING one another. (Galatians 5:19-26)

But **FORNICATION,** and <u>ALL UNCLEANNESS</u>, or <u>COVETOUSNESS</u>, let it not be **o-n-c-e** named among you, as becometh saints; *Neither* <u>FILTHINESS</u>, nor <u>FOOLISH TALKING</u>, nor

JESTING, which are not convenient: but rather giving of thanks  For this ye know, that no **WHOREMONGER,** nor UNCLEAN PERSON, nor COVETOUS MAN, who is an IDOLATER, HATH A-N-Y INHERITANCE IN THE KINGDOM OF CHRIST AND OF GOD. LET NO MAN DECEIVE YOU WITH VAIN WORDS; *for b-e-c-a-u-s-e* OF THESE THINGS COMETH THE W-R-A-T-H O-F G-O-D UPON THE CHILDREN OF D-I-S-O-B-E-D-I-E-N-C-E. Be not ye therefore partakers with them. (Ephesians 5:3-7)

Set your affection on things *above*, NOT on things on the earth.  For ye are D-E-A-D, and your life is hid with Christ in God.  When Christ, who is our life, shall appear, then shall ye also appear with him in glory.  M-O-R-T-I-F-Y (D-E-N-Y) therefore your members which are upon the earth; **FORNICATION,** UNCLEANNESS, INORDINATE AFFECTION, EVIL CONCUPISCENCE, and COVETOUSNESS, which is IDOLATRY: For which things' sake the W-R-A-T-H O-F G-O-D cometh on the CHILDREN OF DISOBEDIENCE:  In the which ye also walked some time, when ye lived in them. But now ye also "PUT OFF" all these; ANGER, WRATH, MALICE, BLASPHEMY, FILTHY COMMUNICATION OUT OF YOUR MOUTH. LIE NOT one to another, seeing that ye have "PUT OFF" the old man with his deeds; (Colossians 3:2-9)

Furthermore then we beseech you, brethren, and exhort you by the Lord Jesus, that as ye have received of us how ye O-U-G-H-T to walk (live) and *to please God,* so ye would abound more and more.  For ye know what C-O-M-M-A-N-D-M-E-N-T-S we gave you by the Lord Jesus.  For this is the will of God, even your sanctification,  that ye should A-B-S-T-A-I-N FROM **FORNICATION:** That every one of you should know how to POSSESS (CONTROL) his vessel in sanctification and honour;  N-O-T in the lust of CONCUPISCENCE (STRONG SEXUAL DESIRES), even as the Gentiles which know not God:  That no man go beyond and defraud his brother in any matter: *because* that THE LORD IS THE AVENGER OF ALL SUCH, as we also have forewarned you and testified.  For God hath N-O-T CALLED US UNTO UNCLEANNESS, *but unto holiness.* (1 Thessalonians 4:1-7)

Knowing this, that the law is *not* made for a righteous man, *b-u-t* for the LAWLESS and DISOBEDIENT, for the UNGODLY and for SINNERS, for UNHOLY and PROFANE, for MURDERERS of fathers and murderers of mothers, for MANSLAYERS for **WHOREMONGERS,** for them that DEFILE THEMSELVES WITH MANKIND, for MENSTEALERS, for LIARS, for PERJURED PERSONS, and if there be any other thing that is CONTRARY TO SOUND DOCTRINE; (1 Timothy 1:9-10)

Looking D-I-L-I-G-E-N-T-L-Y lest any man fail of the grace of God; lest any root of bitterness springing up trouble you, and thereby many be defiled;  Lest there be any **FORNICATOR,** or PROFANCE PERSON, as Esau, who for one morsel of meat sold his birthright.  For ye know how that afterward, when he would have inherited the blessing, HE WAS R-E-J-E-C-T-E-D: for he found NO PLACE OF REPENTANCE, **though he sought it carefully with tears.**  (Hebrews 12:15-17)

Marriage is honourable in all, and the bed undefiled:  *b-u-t*  **WHOREMONGERS** and **ADULTERERS** God will judge.  (Hebrews 13:4)

If ye fulfil the ROYAL LAW according to the scripture, *Thou shalt love thy neighbour as thyself, ye do well:*  *B-u-t* IF YE HAVE RESPECT (DISCRIMINATION) TO PERSONS, YE COMMIT SINS, and ARE CONVINCED OF THE LAW AS TRANSGRESSORS.  For whosoever shall keep the whole law, and *yet* OFFEND IN ONE POINT, HE IS GUILTY OF ALL.  For he that said, DO NOT COMMIT **ADULTERY,** said also, DO NOT KILL. Now if thou commit *no* adultery, yet if thou KILL, thou art become a transgressor of the law. (James 2:8-11)

# Ye <u>ADULTERERS</u> and <u>ADULTERESSES</u>, know ye not that the friendship of the "WORLD" is E-N-M-I-T-Y (HOSTILITY) with God?

# whosoever therefore will be a friend of the "WORLD" is the ENEMY OF GOD.

(James 4:4)

But chiefly them that WALK (LIVE) AFTER THE FLESH (SIN) in the LUST OF UNCLEANNESS, and DESPISE GOVERNMENT (SPIRITUAL LEADERSHIP). PRESUMPTUOUS are they, SELFWILLED, they are NOT AFRAID TO SPEAK EVIL OF DIGNITIES. Whereas angels, which are greater in power and might, bring not railing accusation against them before the Lord. But these, as natural brute beasts, **made to be taken and d-e-s-t-r-o-y-e-d,** SPEAK EVIL OF THE THINGS THAT THEY UNDERSTAND NOT; and shall UTTERLY PERISH IN THEIR OWN CORRUPTION; And shall receive the REWARD OF UNRIGHTEOUSNESS, as they that count it PLEASURE TO RIOT in the day time. Spots they are and blemishes, sporting themselves with their own deceivings while they feast with you; Having EYES FULL OF **ADULTERY** and that CANNOT CEASE FROM SIN; beguiling unstable souls: an heart they have exercised with covetous practices; C-U-R-S-E-D C-H-I-L-D-R-E-N: Which have FORSAKEN THE RIGHT WAY, and ARE GONE ASTRAY, following the way of Balaam the son of Bosor, who LOVED THE WAGES OF UNRIGHTEOUSNESS; But was rebuked for his

33

iniquity: the dumb ass speaking with man's voice forbad the madness of the prophet. These are wells without water, clouds that are carried with a tempest; **to whom the mist of darkness is reserved for ever.** For when they speak great SWELLING WORDS OF VANITY, they allure through the LUSTS OF THE FLESH, through MUCH WANTONNESS, those that were clean escaped from them who live in error. While they promise them liberty, they themselves are the S-E-R-V-A-N-T-S O-F C-O-R-R-U-P-T-I-O-N: for of whom a man is OVERCOME, of the same is he brought in BONDAGE. For if *after* they have escaped the pollutions of the world through the knowledge of the Lord and Saviour Jesus Christ, they are again ENTANGLED therein, and OVERCOME, the latter end is **worse** with them than the beginning. **For it had been better for them not to have known the way of righteousness, than, after they have known it, to t-u-r-n (away) from the holy commandment delivered unto them.** But it is happened unto them according to the true proverb, THE DOG IS TURNED TO HIS OWN VOMIT AGAIN; and THE SOW THAT WAS WASHED (HAS TURNED) TO HER WALLOWING IN THE MIRE. (2 Peter 2:10-22)

Beloved, when I gave all diligence to write unto you of the common salvation, it was needful for me to write unto you, and exhort you that YE SHOULD E-A-R-N-E-S-T-L-Y C-O-N-T-E-N-D FOR THE FAITH which was once delivered unto the saints. For there are certain men crept in unawares, who were before of old ordained to this condemnation, ungodly men, TURNING THE GRACE OF OUR GOD INTO LASCIVIOUSNESS (LEWD

BEHAVIOR), *and* denying the only Lord God, and our Lord Jesus Christ. I will therefore put you in REMEMBRANCE, though ye once knew this, how that the Lord, having saved the people out of the land of Egypt, afterward **d-e-s-t-r-o-y-e-d them that believed not.** *A-n-d* the angels which kept not their first estate, but left their own habitation, he hath **reserved in everlasting chains under darkness unto the judgment of the great day.** Even as Sodom and Gomorrha, and the cities about them in like manner, giving themselves over to **FORNICATION** (ANY SEXUAL ACTIVITY OUTSIDE OF A MALE/FEMALE MARRIAGE COVENANT), and going after strange flesh, are set forth for an EXAMPLE, **suffering the vengeance of eternal fire.** Likewise also these **filthy dreamers** DEFILE THE FLESH, DESPISE DOMINION (SPIRITUAL SUPERVISION), and SPEAK EVIL OF DIGNITIES. Yet Michael the archangel, when contending with the devil he disputed about the body of Moses, durst not bring against him a railing accusation, but said, **The Lord rebuke thee.** But these speak evil of those things which they know *not:* but what they know naturally, as BRUTE BEASTS, in those things they corrupt themselves. Woe unto them! for they have gone in the way of Cain, and ran greedily after the error of Balaam for reward, and perished in the gainsaying of Core. These are spots in your feasts of charity, when they feast with you, feeding themselves without fear: clouds they are without water, carried about of winds; trees whose fruit withereth, without fruit, twice dead, plucked up by the roots; Raging waves of the sea, foaming out their own shame; wandering stars, **to whom is reserved the blackness of darkness for ever.** And *Enoch* also, the seventh from Adam, prophesied of these, saying, BEHOLD, THE LORD COMETH WITH TEN THOUSAND OF HIS SAINTS, TO EXECUTE JUDGMENT UPON ALL, and TO CONVINCE ALL THAT ARE UNGODLY AMONG THEM OF ALL THEIR UNGODLY DEEDS WHICH THEY HAVE UNGODLY COMMITTED, and OF ALL THEIR HARD SPEECHES WHICH UNGOLDY SINNERS HAVE SPOKEN AGAINST HIM. THESE ARE MURMURERS, COMPLAINERS, WALKING AFTER THEIR OWN LUSTS; and THEIR MOUTH SPEAKETH GREAT SWELLING WORDS, HAVING MEN'S PERSONS IN ADMIRATION BECAUSE OF ADVANTAGE. But, beloved, *remember* ye the words which were spoken before of the apostles of our Lord Jesus Christ; How that they told you THERE SHOULD BE MOCKERS IN THE LAST TIME, WHO SHOULD WALK AFTER THEIR OWN UNGODLY LUSTS. THESE BE THEY WHO S-E-P-A-R-A-T-E    T-H-E-M-S-E-L-V-E-S, SENSUAL, HAVING NOT THE SPIRIT. (Jude 1:3-19)

And to the angel of the church in Pergamos write; *These things saith he (Jesus) which hath the sharp sword with two edges;* I know thy works, and where thou dwellest, even where Satan's seat is: and thou holdest fast my name, and hast not denied my faith, even in those days wherein Antipas was my faithful martyr, who was slain among you, where Satan dwelleth. *B-u-t* I HAVE A FEW THINGS AGAINST THEE, because thou hast there them that hold THE DOCTRINE OF BALAAM, who taught Balac to cast a stumblingblock before the children of Israel, <u>to eat things sacrificed unto idols</u>, and to commit **FORNICATION.** So hast thou also them that hold the DOCTRINE OF THE NICOLAITANES (GENERALLY, A SELF INDULGENT LIFESTYLE, ESPECIALLY SEXUALLY, *and* EATING FOOD SACRIFICED TO IDOLS) AND, WHICH THING I H-A-T-E. R-E-P-E-N-T; *or else* <u>I will come unto thee quickly, and will fight against them with the sword of my mouth</u>. *He that hath an ear, let him hear what the Spirit saith unto the churches;* To him that O-V-E-R-C-O-M-E-T-H will I give to eat of the <u>hidden manna</u>, and will give him a <u>white stone</u>, and in the stone a <u>new name</u> written, which no man knoweth saving he that receiveth it. And unto the angel of the church in <u>Thyatira</u> write; *These things saith the Son of God, who hath his eyes like unto a flame of fire, and his feet are like fine brass;* I know thy <u>works</u>, and charity, and <u>service</u>, and <u>faith</u>, and thy <u>patience</u>, and thy <u>works</u>; and the last to be more than the first. *N-o-t-w-i-t-h-s-t-a-n-d-i-n-g* I HAVE A FEW THINGS AGAINST THEE, *because* <u>thou sufferest that woman Jezebel</u>, which calleth herself a prophetess, <u>to teach and to seduce my servants</u> to commit **FORNICATION,** *and* TO EAT THINGS SACRIFICED UNTO IDOLS. And <u>I gave her space to repent of her **FORNICATION**</u>; *a-n-d (b-u-t)* she repented N-O-T. **Behold, I will cast her into a bed, *and* them that commit ADULTERY with her into g-r-e-a-t t-r-i-b-u-l-a-t-i-o-n,** *except* **they <u>repent of their deeds</u>.** *And* I WILL KILL HER CHILDREN WITH DEATH; and all the churches shall know that (...............)

# I AM HE WHICH

# S-E-A-R-C-H-E-T-H

# THE REINS

# *and*

# HEARTS:

# *and*

# I WILL GIVE UNTO EVERY ONE OF YOU ACCORDING TO YOUR W-O-R-K-S.

But unto you I say, and unto the rest in Thyatira, as many as have *not* this doctrine, and which have *not* known the depths of Satan, as they speak; *I will put upon you none other burden.* But that which ye have already HOLD FAST TILL I COME. And he that O-V-E-R-C-O-M-E-T-H, *and* KEEPETH MY WORKS UNTO THE END, *to him will I give power over the nations:* And he shall rule them with a rod of iron; as the vessels of a potter shall they be broken to shivers: even as I received of my Father. And I will give him the morning star. HE THAT HATH AN EAR, LET HIM HEAR WHAT

THE SPIRIT SAITH UNTO THE CHURCHES. (Revelation 2:12-29)

And the sixth angel sounded, and I heard a voice from the four horns of the golden altar which is before God, Saying to the sixth angel which had the trumpet, LOOSE THE FOUR ANGELS WHICH ARE BOUND IN THE GREAT RIVER EUPHRATES. And the four angels were loosed, which were prepared for an hour, and a day, and a month, and a year, for TO SLAY THE THIRD PART OF MEN. And the number of the army of the horsemen were two hundred thousand thousand: and I heard the number of them. And thus I saw the horses in the vision, and them that sat on them, having breastplates of fire, and of jacinth, and brimstone: and the heads of the horses were as the heads of lions; and out of their mouths issued fire and smoke and brimstone. BY THESE THREE WAS A THIRD PART OF MEN KILLED, BY THE FIRE, and BY THE SMOKE, and BY THE BRIMSTONE, WHICH ISSUED OUT OF THEIR MOUTHS. For their power is in their mouth, and in their tails: for their tails were like unto serpents, and had heads, and with them they do hurt. And THE REST OF THE MEN WHICH WERE NOT KILLED BY THESE PLAGUES YET REPENTED NOT OF THE WORKS OF THEIR HANDS, THAT THEY SHOULD NOT WORSHIP DEVILS, and IDOLS of gold, and silver, and brass, and stone, and of wood: which neither can see, nor hear, nor walk: *N-e-i-t-h-e-r* REPENTED THEY OF THEIR MURDERS, NOR OF THEIR SORCERIES, NOR OF THEIR **FORNICATION,** NOR OF THEIR THEFTS. (Revelation 9:13-21)

*And I saw a new heaven and a new earth: for the first heaven and the first earth were passed away; and there was no more sea.* And I John saw THE HOLY CITY, NEW JERUSALEM, coming down from God out of heaven, prepared as a bride adorned for her husband. And I heard a great voice out of heaven saying, BEHOLD, THE TABERNACLE OF GOD IS WITH MEN, and HE WILL DWELL WITH THEM, and THEY SHALL BE HIS PEOPLE, and GOD HIMSELF SHALL BE WITH THEM, and BE THEIR GOD. *And God shall wipe away all tears from their eyes; and there shall be no more death, neither sorrow, nor crying, neither shall there be any more pain: for the former things are passed away. And he that sat upon the throne said, Behold, I make all things new.* And he said unto me, Write: for these words are true and faithful. And he said unto me, It is done. I am Alpha and Omega, the beginning and the end. I will give unto him that is athirst of the fountain of the water of life freely. He that O-V-E-R- C-O-M-E-T-H shall inherit *all* things; and I WILL BE HIS GOD, and HE SHALL BE MY SON. ***B-u-t*** the FEARFUL, and <u>UNBELIEVING</u>, and <u>THE ABOMINABLE</u>, and <u>MURDERERS</u>, and **WHOREMONGERS,** and <u>SORCERERS</u>, and <u>IDOLATERS</u>, and <u>ALL L-I-A-R-S</u>, SHALL HAVE THEIR PART IN THE LAKE WHICH BURNETH WITH FIRE and BRIMSTONE: which is the second death. (Revelation 21:1-8)

He that is UNJUST, let him be unjust still: and he which is FILTHY, let him be filthy still: and he that *is righteous,* let him be righteous still: and he that is *holy,* let him be holy still. And, BEHOLD, I COME QUICKLY; and MY REWARD IS WITH ME, TO

GIVE EVERY MAN ACCORDING AS HIS WORK SHALL BE. I am Alpha and Omega, the beginning and the end, the first and the last. Blessed are they that "DO" his commandments, that they may have right to the tree of life, and may enter in through the gates into the city. For W-I-T-H-O-U-T are DOGS, and SORCERERS, and **WHOREMONGERS,** and MURDERERS, and IDOLATERS, and WHOSOEVER LOVETH and MAKETH A LIE. (Revelation 22:11-15)

# SPIRITUAL

## OLD TESTAMENT

Then I will set my face against that man, and against his family, and will cut him off, and all that go a **WHORING** after him, to commit **WHOREDOM** with Molech, from among their people. (Leviticus 20:5)

And the LORD spake unto Moses and unto Aaron, saying, How long shall I bear with this evil congregation, which murmur against me? I have heard the murmurings of the children of Israel, which they murmur against me. Say unto them, As truly as I live, saith the LORD, as ye have spoken in mine ears, SO WILL I DO TO YOU: YOUR CARCASES SHALL FALL IN THIS WILDERNESS; and all that were numbered of you, according to your whole number, from twenty years old and upward which have murmured against me. Doubtless ye shall not come into the land, concerning which I sware to make you dwell therein, save Caleb the son of Jephunneh, and Joshua the son of Nun. *But* your little ones, which ye said should be a prey, them will I bring in, and they shall know the LAND which ye have despised. But as for you, your carcases, they shall fall in this wilderness. And your children shall wander in the wilderness forty years, and bear your **WHOREDOMS,** *until* your carcases be wasted in the wilderness. After the number of the days in which ye searched the land, **even forty days, each**

**day for a year,** SHALL YE BEAR YOUR INIQUITIES, EVEN FORTY YEARS, and ye shall know my breach of promise. I the LORD have said, I will surely do it unto all this evil congregation, that are gathered together against me: in this wilderness they shall be consumed, and there they shall die. And the men, which Moses sent to search the land, who returned, and made all the congregation to murmur against him, by bringing up a slander upon the land, **Even those men that did bring up the evil report upon the land,** DIED BY THE PLAGUE BEFORE THE LORD. (Numbers 14:26-37)

And Israel abode in Shittim, and the people began to commit **WHOREDOM** with the daughters of Moab. And they called the people unto the SACRIFICES OF THEIR GODS: and the people did eat, and BOWED DOWN TO THEIR GODS. And Israel joined himself unto Baalpeor: **and the anger of the LORD was kindled against Israel.** And the LORD said unto Moses, Take all the HEADS of the people, and HANG THEM up before the LORD against the sun, that the F-I-E-R-C-E ANGER OF THE LORD may be turned away from Israel. And Moses said unto the judges of Israel, **Slay ye every one his men that were joined unto Baalpeor.** And, behold, one of the children of Israel came and brought unto his brethren a Midianitish woman in the sight of Moses, and in the sight of all the congregation of the children of Israel, who were weeping before the door of the tabernacle of the congregation. And when PHINEHAS, the son of Eleazar, the son of Aaron the priest, saw it, he rose up from among the congregation, and took a javelin in his hand; And he went after the man of Israel into the tent, and thrust both of them through, the man of Israel, and the woman through her belly. *So the plague was stayed from the children of Israel.* And those that died in the plague were twenty and four thousand (24,000). And the LORD spake unto Moses, saying, Phinehas, the son of Eleazar, the son of Aaron the priest, hath turned my wrath away from the children of Israel, while he was zealous for my sake among them, that I consumed not the children of Israel in my jealousy. (Numbers 25:1-11)

And it came to pass, when Joram saw Jehu, that he said, Is it peace, Jehu? And he answered, What peace, so long as the **WHOREDOMS (IDOLATRY)** of thy mother Jezebel and her witchcrafts are so many? (2 Kings 9:22)

In his days the EDOMITES revolted from under the dominion of Judah, and made themselves a king. Then JEHORAM went forth with his princes, and all his chariots with him: and he rose up by night, and smote the Edomites which compassed him in, and the captains of the chariots. So the Edomites revolted from under the hand of Judah unto this day. The same time also did LIBNAH revolt from under his hand; because he had forsaken the LORD God of his fathers. Moreover he (Libnah) made HIGH PLACES in the mountains of Judah and caused the inhabitants of Jerusalem to commit **FORNICATION,** and compelled Judah thereto. And there came a writing to him from Elijah the prophet, saying, Thus saith the LORD God of David thy father, *Because* thou hast not walked in the ways of Jehoshaphat thy father, nor in the ways of Asa king of Judah, But hast walked in the way of

45

the kings of Israel, and hast made Judah and the inhabitants of Jerusalem to go a **WHORING,** like to the **WHOREDOMS** of the house of Ahab, and also hast slain thy brethren of thy father's house, *which were better than thyself:* Behold, with a GREAT PLAGUE will the LORD smite thy people, and thy children, and thy wives, and all thy goods: And thou shalt have GREAT SICKNESS BY DISEASE OF THY BOWELS, **until thy bowels fall out by reason of the sickness** day by day. Moreover the LORD stirred up against Jehoram the spirit of the Philistines, and of the Arabians, that were near the Ethiopians: And they came up into Judah, and brake into it, and carried away all the substance that was found in the king's house, and his sons also, and his wives; so that there was never a son left him, save Jehoahaz, the youngest of his sons. And after all this the LORD smote him in his bowels with an INCURABLE DISEASE. And it came to pass, that in process of time, after the end of two years, **his bowels fell out by reason of his sickness:** *so* HE DIED OF SORE DISEASES. And his people made no burning for him, like the burning of his fathers. Thirty and two years old was he when he began to reign, and he reigned in Jerusalem eight years, and departed without being desired. Howbeit they buried him in the city of David, but *not* in the sepulchres of the kings. (2 Chronicles 21:8-20)

COME NOW, and LET US REASON TOGETHER, saith the LORD: *though your sins be as scarlet, they shall be as white as snow; though they be red like crimson, they shall be as wool.* **If** ye be W-I-L-L-I-N-G *and* O-B-E-D-I-E-N-T, ye shall eat the good of the land: ***B-u-t if*** YE REFUSE and REBEL, YE SHALL BE DEVOURED WITH THE SWORD: for the mouth of the LORD hath spoken it. How is the faithful city become an **HARLOT!** it *w-a-s* FULL OF JUDGMENT; RIGHTEOUSNESS LODGED IN IT; *but n-o-w* MURDERERS. **Thy silver is become dross, thy wine mixed with water:** Thy princes are REBELLIOUS, and COMPANIONS OF THIEVES: every one loveth gifts, and followeth after rewards: they JUDGE NOT THE FATHERLESS, NEITHER DOTH THE CAUSE OF THE WIDOW COME UNTO THEM. Therefore saith the LORD, the LORD of hosts, the mighty One of Israel, Ah, I WILL EASE ME OF MINE ADVERSARIES, and AVENGE ME OF MINE ENEMIES: *And* I WILL TURN MY HAND UPON THEE, and PURELY P-U-R-G-E AWAY THY DROSS, and TAKE AWAY ALL THY TIN: And I will restore thy judges as at the first, and thy counsellors as at the beginning: *a-f-t-e-r-w-a-r-d* thou shalt be called, *The city of righteousness, the faithful city.* Zion shall be redeemed with JUDGMENT, and her converts with RIGHTEOUSNESS. *And* THE DESTRUCTION OF THE TRANSGRESSORS *and* OF THE SINNERS SHALL BE TOGETHER, and THEY THAT FORSAKE THE LORD SHALL BE C-O-N-S-U-M-E-D. (Isaiah 1:18-28)

And it shall come to pass in that day, that Tyre shall be forgotten seventy years, according to the days of one king: after the end of seventy years shall Tyre sing as an **HARLOT.** Take an harp, go about the city, THOU **HARLOT** THAT HAST BEEN FORGOTTEN; make sweet melody, sing many songs, that thou mayest be remembered. And it shall come to pass after the end of seventy years, that the Lord will visit Tyre, and she shall turn to her hire, and shall commit **FORNICATION** with all the kingdoms of the world upon the face of the earth. (Isaiah 23:15-17)

The righteous perisheth, and no man layeth it to heart: and merciful men are taken away, none considering that T*H*E    R*I*G*H*T*E*O*U*S    I*S    T*A*K*E*N    A*W*A*Y    F*R*O*M    T*H*E    E*V*I*L    T*O    C*O*M*E. He shall enter into peace: they shall rest in their beds, each one walking in his uprightness. *B-u-t* draw near hither, YE SONS OF THE SORCERESS, THE SEED OF THE **ADULTERER** and THE **WHORE.** Against whom do ye sport yourselves? against whom make ye a wide mouth, and draw out the tongue? ARE YE NOT CHILDREN OF TRANSGRESSION, A SEED OF FALSEHOOD. Enflaming yourselves with idols under every green tree, slaying the children in the valleys under the clifts of the rocks? Among the smooth stones of the stream is thy portion; they, they are thy lot: even to them hast thou poured a drink offering, thou hast offered a meat offering. Should I receive comfort in these?  Upon a lofty and high mountain hast thou set thy bed: even thither wentest thou up to offer sacrifice.  Behind the doors also and the posts hast thou set up thy remembrance: for THOU HAS DISCOVERED THYSELF TO A-N-O-T-H-E-R THAN ME, and art gone up; thou hast enlarged thy bed, and made thee a covenant with them; thou lovedst their bed where thou sawest it.   And thou wentest to the king with ointment, and didst increase thy perfumes, and didst send thy messengers far off, and DIDST DEBASE

THYSELF EVEN UNTO HELL. Thou art wearied in the greatness of thy way; yet saidst thou not, There is no hope: thou hast found the life of thine hand; *therefore* **thou wast *not* grieved.** And of whom hast thou been afraid or feared, that thou hast lied, and hast not remembered me, nor laid it to thy heart? HAVE NOT I HELD MY PEACE EVEN OF OLD, and THOU FEAREST ME NOT? I will declare thy righteousness, and thy works; for they shall not profit thee. When thou criest, <u>let thy companies deliver thee</u>; but the wind shall carry them all away; <u>vanity shall take them</u>: but he that putteth his trust in me shall possess the land, and shall inherit *my* holy mountain; And shall say, Cast ye up, cast ye up, prepare the way, take up the stumblingblock out of the way of my people. For thus saith the high and lofty One that inhabiteth eternity, whose name is Holy; I dwell in the high and holy place, WITH HIM ALSO THAT IS OF A CONTRITE and HUMBLE SPIRIT, to *revive* the spirit of the HUMBLE, and to *revive* the heart of the CONTRITE ones. *For* I WILL NOT CONTEND FOR EVER, NEITHER WILL I BE ALWAYS WROTH: for the spirit should fail before me, and the souls which I have made. FOR THE INIQUITY OF HIS C-O-V-E-T-O-U-S-N-E-S-S WAS I WROTH, and SMOTE HIM: I HID ME, and WAS WROTH, and <u>HE WENT ON</u> FROWARDLY (WILLFULLY DISOBEDIENT) IN THE WAY OF HIS HEART. I have seen his ways, and will heal him: I WILL LEAD HIM ALSO, and restore comforts unto him and to his mourners. I create the fruit of the lips; Peace, peace to him that is far off, and to him that is near, saith the LORD; and I will heal him. But the wicked are like the troubled sea, when it cannot rest, whose waters cast up mire and dirt. THERE IS NO PEACE, saith my God, TO THE WICKED. (Isaiah 57:1-21)

T-H-I-N-E  O-W-N  W-I-C-K-E-D-N-E-S-S S-H-A-L-L  C-O-R-R-E-C-T  T-H-E-E, and THY BACKSLIDING SHALL REPROVE THEE: know therefore and see that IT IS AN EVIL THING and BITTER, THAT THOU HAST FORSAKEN THE LORD THY GOD, and **T-H-A-T  M-Y  F-E-A-R I-S  N-O-T  I-N  T-H-E-E,** saith the Lord GOD of hosts. For of old time I have broken thy yoke, and burst thy bands; and thou saidst, I WILL NOT TRANSGRESS; when upon every high hill and under every green tree thou wanderest, PLAYING THE **HARLOT.** Yet I had planted thee a noble vine, wholly a *right* seed: how then art thou t-u-r-n-e-d into the D-E-G-E-N-E-R-A-T-E  P-L-A-N-T of a strange vine unto me? For though thou wash thee with nitre, and take thee much soap, YET THINE INIQUITY IS MARKED BEFORE ME, saith the Lord GOD. (Jeremiah 2:19-22)

They say, If a man put away his wife, and she go from him, and become another man's, shall he return unto her again? shall not that land be greatly polluted? but THOU HAST PLAYED THE **HARLOT** WITH MANY LOVERS; Y-E-T RETURN AGAIN TO ME, saith the LORD. Lift up thine eyes unto the HIGH PLACES, and see where thou hast not been lien with. In the ways hast thou sat for them, as the Arabian in the wilderness; and THOU HAST POLLUTED THE LAND WITH THY **WHOREDOMS** and WITH THY WICKEDNESS. *T-h-e-r-e-f-o-r-e* **the showers have been withholden, and there hath been no**

50

**latter rain;** and thou hadst a **WHORE'S** forehead, **thou refusedst to be ashamed.** Wilt thou not from this time cry unto me, My father, thou art the guide of my youth? WILL HE RESERVE HIS ANGER FOR EVER? will he keep it to the end? Behold, thou hast spoken and done evil things as thou couldest. The LORD said also unto me in the days of Josiah the king, Hast thou seen that which BACKSLIDING ISRAEL hath done? she is gone up upon every high mountain and under every green tree, and there hath PLAYED THE **HARLOT.** And I said after she had done all these things, TURN THOU UNTO ME. *B-u-t* SHE RETURNED N-O-T. And her treacherous sister Judah saw it. And I saw, when for all the causes whereby BACKSLIDING ISRAEL COMMITTED **ADULTERY** I had put her away, and given her a bill of divorce; yet her treacherous sister JUDAH feared not, but went and played the HARLOT also. And it came to pass through the lightness of her **WHOREDOME,** that she defiled the land, and committed **ADULTERY** with stones and with stocks. And *yet* for ALL this her treacherous sister Judah hath *not* turned unto me with her whole heart, but feignedly, saith the LORD. And the LORD said unto me, The backsliding Israel hath justified herself more than treacherous Judah. Go and proclaim these words toward the north, and say, RETURN, THOU BACKSLIDING ISRAEL, saith the LORD; and I will *not* cause mine anger to fall upon you: for I AM MERCIFUL, saith the LORD, *and* I WILL NOT KEEP ANGER FOR EVER. ONLY ACKNOWLEDGE THINE INIQUITY, THAT THOU HAST TRANSGRESSED AGAINST THE LORD THY GOD, and HAST SCATTERED THY WAYS TO THE

STRANGERS UNDER EVERY GREEN TREE, and YE HAVE NOT OBEYED MY VOICE, saith the LORD. TURN, O BACKSLIDING CHILDREN, saith the LORD; *for* I A*M M*A*R*R*I*E*D U*N*T*O Y*O*U: and I will take you one of a city, and two of a family, and I will bring you to Zion: And I will give you PASTORS according to mine heart, which shall feed you with knowledge and understanding. And it shall come to pass, when ye be multiplied and increased in the land, in those days, saith the LORD, they shall say no more, The ark of the covenant of the LORD: neither shall it come to mind: neither shall they remember it; neither shall they visit it; neither shall that be done any more. At that time they shall call Jerusalem the throne of the LORD; and all the nations shall be gathered unto it, to the name of the LORD, to Jerusalem: **neither shall they walk any more after the imagination of their evil heart.** In those days the house of Judah shall walk with the house of Israel, and they shall come together out of the land of the north to the land that I have given for an inheritance unto your fathers. But I said, How shall I put thee among the children, and give thee a pleasant land, a goodly heritage of the hosts of nations? and I said, Thou shalt call me, My father; and shalt not turn away from me. SURELY AS A WIFE TREACHEROUSLY DEPARTETH FROM HER HUSBAND, SO HAVE YE DEALT TREACHEROUSLY WITH ME, O house of Israel, saith the LORD. A voice was heard upon the high places, weeping and supplications of the children of Israel: for THEY HAVE PERVERTED THEIR WAY, and THEY HAVE FORGOTTEN THE LORD THEIR GOD. R-E-T-U-R-N, ye backsliding children, and I will heal your backslidings. Behold, we come unto thee; for thou art the LORD our God. Truly in vain is salvation hoped for from the hills, and from the multitude of mountains: TRULY IN THE LORD OUR GOD IS THE SALVATION OF ISRAEL. For shame hath devoured the labour of our fathers from our youth; their flocks and their herds, their sons and their daughters. We lie down in our shame, and our confusion covereth us: for WE HAVE SINNED AGAINST THE LORD OUR GOD, WE and OUR FATHER, FROM OUR YOUTH EVEN UNTO THIS DAY, and HAVE NOT OBEYED THE VOICE OF THE LORD OUR GOD. (Jeremiah 3:1-25)

How shall I pardon thee for this? **thy children have forsaken me,** and SWORN BY THEM THAT ARE NO GODS: when I had fed them to the full, they then committed **ADULTERY,** and assembled themselves by troops in the **HARLOT'S** HOUSES. (Jeremiah 5:7)

Behold, ye trust in *lying* words, that cannot profit. Will ye STEAL, MURDER, and COMMIT **ADULTERY,** and SWEAR FALSELY, and BURN INCENSE UNTO BAAL. and WALK AFTER OTHER GODS WHOM YE KNOW NOT; And come and stand before *me* in this house, which is called by my name, and say, WE ARE DELIVERED TO DO ALL THESE A-B-O-M-I-N-A-T-I-O-N-S? Is this house, which is called by my name, become a den of robbers in your eyes? Behold, even I have seen it, saith the LORD. (Jeremiah 7:8-11)

Oh that my head were waters, and mine eyes a fountain of tears, that I might weep day and night for the SLAIN of the daughter of my people! Oh that I had in the wilderness a lodging place of wayfaring men; that I might leave my people, and go from them! for THEY BE ALL **ADULTERERS,** an assembly of treacherous men. *And* they bend their tongues like their bow for LIES: but **they are not valiant for the truth upon the earth;** for THEY PROCEED FROM EVIL TO EVIL, *and* they know not me, saith the LORD. Take ye heed every one of his neighbour, and trust ye not in any brother: for every brother will utterly SUPPLANT, and every neighbour will walk with SLANDERS. *And* they will DECEIVE every one his neighbour, *and* will not speak the truth: they have taught their tongue to speak LIES, and weary themselves to commit iniquity. Thine habitation is in the midst of DECEIT; through DECEIT THEY REFUSE TO KNOW ME, saith the LORD. Therefore thus saith the LORD of hosts, BEHOLD, I WILL M-E-L-T THEM, and T-R-Y THEM; for how shall I do for the daughter of my people? Their tongue is as an arrow shot out; it speaketh DECEIT: one speaketh peaceably to his neighbour with his mouth, but in *heart* he layeth his wait. Shall I not visit them for these things? saith the LORD: shall not my soul be avenged on such a nation as this? For the mountains will I take up a weeping and wailing, and for the habitations of the wilderness a lamentation, because they are burned up, so that none can pass through them; neither can men hear the voice of the cattle; both the fowl of the heavens and the beast are fled; they are gone. And I will make Jerusalem heaps, and A DEN OF DRAGONS; and I will make the cities of Judah desolate, without an inhabitant. Who is the wise man, that may understand this? and who is he to whom the mouth of the LORD hath spoken, that he may declare it, for what the land perisheth and is burned up like a wilderness, that none passeth through? And the LORD saith, *B-e-c-a-u-s-e* THEY HAVE FORSAKEN MY L-A-W WHICH I SET BEFORE THEM, *and* HAVE N-O-T O-B-E-Y-E-D MY VOICE, NEITHER WALKED THEREIN; But have WALKED AFTER THE IMAGINATION OF THEIR OWN HEART, and after Baalim, which their fathers taught them: Therefore thus saith the LORD of hosts, the God of Israel; Behold, I will feed them, even this people, with WORMWOOD, and give them water of GALL to drink. I will scatter them also among the heathen, whom neither they nor their fathers have known: and I WILL SEND A SWORD AFTER THEM, till I have consumed them. Thus saith the LORD of hosts, **Consider ye,** and call for the mourning women, that they may come; and send for cunning women, that they may come: And let them make haste, and take up a wailing for us, that our eyes may run down with tears, and our eyelids gush out with waters. For a voice of wailing is heard out of Zion, How are we spoiled! we are greatly confounded, because we have forsaken the land, because our dwellings have cast us out. *Yet* hear the word of the LORD, O ye women, and let your ear receive the word of his mouth, and teach your daughters wailing, and every one her neighbour lamentation. For death is come up into our windows, and is entered into our palaces, to cut off the children from without, and the young men from the streets. Speak, THUS SAITH THE LORD, Even the carcases of men shall fall as dung upon the open field, and as the handful after the harvestman, and none shall gather them. THUS SAITH THE LORD, LET NOT THE WISE MAN GLORY IN HIS WISDOM, NEITHER LET THE MIGHTY MAN GLORY IN HIS MIGHT, LET NOT THE RICH MAN GLORY IN HIS RICHES: *But let him that glorieth glory in this, that he understandeth and knoweth me, that I am the LORD which exercise lovingkindness, judgment, and righteousness, in the earth: for in these things I delight, saith the LORD.* Behold, the days come, saith the LORD, that I will punish all them which are circumcised w-i-t-h the *un*circumcised; Egypt, and Judah, and Edom, and the children of Ammon, and Moab, and all that are in the utmost corners, that dwell in the wilderness: for ALL these nations are *un*circumcised, and ALL the house of Israel are UNCIRCUMCISED IN THE H-E-A-R-T. (Jeremiah 9:1-26)

I have seen thine **ADULTERIES,** and thy neighings, the lewdness of thy **WHOREDOME,** and thine ABOMINATIONS on the hills in the fields. Woe unto thee, O Jerusalem! wilt thou not be made clean? when shall it once be? (Jeremiah 13:27)

WOE BE UNTO THE PASTORS that destroy and scatter the sheep of my pasture! saith the LORD. Therefore thus saith the LORD God of Israel AGAINST THE PASTORS that feed my people; **Ye have scattered my flock, and driven them away, and have not visited them:** behold, I WILL VISIT UPON YOU THE EVIL OF YOUR DOINGS, saith the LORD. *And I will gather the remnant of my flock out of all countries whither I have driven them, and will bring them again to their*

56

*folds; and they shall be fruitful and increase.* And I will set up SHEPHERDS over them which shall feed them: and they shall <u>fear no more,</u> <u>nor be dismayed,</u> <u>neither shall they be lacking,</u> saith the LORD. Behold, the days come, saith the LORD, that I will raise unto David a righteous Branch, and a King shall reign and prosper, and shall execute judgment and justice in the earth. In his days Judah shall be saved, and Israel shall dwell safely: and this is his name whereby he shall be called, THE LORD OUR RIGHTEOUSNESS. Therefore, behold, the days come, saith the LORD, that they shall no more say, The LORD liveth, which brought up the children of Israel out of the land of Egypt; But, The LORD liveth, which brought up and which led the seed of the house of Israel out of the north country, and from all countries whither I had driven them; and they shall dwell in their own land. MINE HEART WITHIN ME IS BROKEN BECAUSE OF THE PROPHETS; all my bones shake; I am like a drunken man, and like a man whom wine hath overcome, *because* of the LORD, and *because* of the words of his holiness. FOR THE LAND IS FULL OF **ADULTERERS;** for because of SWEARING the land mourneth; the pleasant places of the wilderness are dried up, and <u>THEIR COURSE IS EVIL,</u> and their force is not right. **For both prophet and priest are profane;** yea, *i-n m-y h-o-u-s-e* have I found their wickedness, saith the LORD. Wherefore their way shall be unto them as slippery ways in the darkness: they shall be driven on, and fall therein: for I WILL BRING EVIL UPON THEM, even the year of their visitation, saith the LORD. And I have seen folly in the <u>prophets of Samaria</u>; they prophesied in Baal, and caused my people Israel to err. I have seen also in the <u>prophets</u>

57

of Jerusalem an horrible thing: THEY COMMIT **ADULTERY,** and WALK IN LIES: they strengthen also the hands of evildoers, that **none doth return from his wickedness;** they are all of them unto me as SODOM, and the inhabitants thereof as GOMORRAH. Therefore thus saith the LORD of hosts concerning the prophets; Behold, I WILL FEED THEM WITH WORMWOOD, and MAKE THEM DRINK THE WATER OF GALL: for from the prophets of Jerusalem is profaneness gone forth into all the land. Thus saith the LORD of hosts, HEARKEN NOT UNTO THE WORDS OF THE PROPHETS THAT PROPHESY UNTO YOU: THEY MAKE YOU VAIN: THEY SPEAK A VISION OF THEIR O-W-N HEART, and N-O-T OUT OF THE MOUTH OF THE LORD. They say still unto them that despise me, The LORD hath said, **Ye shall have peace; and they say unto every one that walketh after the imagination of his own heart, No evil shall come upon you.** For who hath stood in the counsel of the LORD, and hath perceived and heard his word? who hath marked his word, and heard it? Behold, A WHIRLWIND OF THE LORD IS GONE FORTH IN FURY, EVEN A GRIEVOUS WHIRLWIND: IT SHALL FALL GRIEVOUSLY UPON THE HEAD OF THE WICKED. THE ANGER OF THE LORD SHALL NOT RETURN, UNTIL HE HAVE EXECUTED, and TILL HE HAVE PERFORMED THE THOUGHTS OF HIS HEART: in the latter days ye shall consider it perfectly. I have **not** sent these prophets, *yet* they ran: I have **not** spoken to them, *yet* they prophesied. But *if* they had STOOD IN MY COUNSEL, and had CAUSED MY PEOPLE TO HEAR MY WORDS, then THEY SHOULD HAVE TURNED THEM FROM THEIR EVIL

WAY, and FROM THE EVIL OF THEIR DOINGS. Am I a God at hand, saith the LORD, and not a God afar off? Can any hide himself in secret places that I shall not see him? saith the LORD. Do not I fill heaven and earth? saith the LORD. I have heard what the prophets said, that PROPHESY LIES IN MY NAME, saying, I have dreamed, I have dreamed. How long shall this be in the heart of the prophets that prophesy lies? yea, they are prophets of the DECEIT OF THEIR O-W-N HEART; Which think to cause my people to forget my name by their dreams which they tell every man to his neighbour, as their fathers have forgotten my name for Baal. The prophet that hath a dream, let him tell a dream; and he that hath my word, let him speak my word faithfully. What is the chaff to the wheat? saith the LORD. Is not *my word* like as a F-I-R-E? saith the LORD; and like a H-A-M-M-E-R that breaketh the rock in pieces? Therefore, behold, I am **a-g-a-i-n-s-t** the prophets, saith the LORD, that steal my words every one from his neighbour. Behold, I am **against** the prophets, saith the LORD, that use their tongues, and say, He saith. Behold, I am **against** them that prophesy false dreams, saith the LORD, and do tell them, and CAUSE MY PEOPLE TO ERR BY THEIR LIES, and BY THEIR LIGHTNESS; *yet* **I sent them not**, nor commanded them: *therefore* THEY SHALL NOT PROFIT THIS PEOPLE A-T A-L-L, saith the LORD. And when this people, or the prophet, or a priest, shall ask thee, saying, What is the burden of the LORD? thou shalt then say unto them, What burden? I WILL EVEN FORSAKE YOU, saith the LORD. And as for the prophet, and the priest, and the people, that shall say, The burden of the LORD, I will even punish that man and his house. Thus shall ye say every one to his neighbour, and every one to his brother, What hath the LORD answered? and, What hath the LORD spoken? And the burden of the LORD shall ye mention no more: **for every man's word shall be his b-u-r-d-e-n;** *for* **YE HAVE PERVERTED THE WORDS OF THE LIVING GOD,** of the LORD of hosts our God. Thus shalt thou say to the prophet, What hath the LORD answered thee? and, What hath the LORD spoken? But since ye say, The burden of the LORD; therefore thus saith the LORD; Because ye say this word, The burden of the LORD, and I have sent unto you, saying, Ye shall NOT say, The burden of the LORD; Therefore, behold, **I, EVEN I, WILL UTTERLY FORGET YOU, and I WILL FORSAKE YOU,** and the city that I gave you and your fathers, and cast you out of my presence: *And* I WILL BRING AN EVERLASTING REPROACH UPON YOU, and A PERPETUAL SHAME, WHICH SHALL NOT BE FORGOTTEN. (Jeremiah 23:1-40)

Again the word of the Lord came unto me, saying, Son of man, cause Jerusalem to know her A-B-O-M-I-N-A-T-I-O-N-S, And say, Thus saith the Lord God unto Jerusalem; Thy birth and thy nativity is of the land of Canaan; thy father was an Amorite, and thy mother an Hittite. And as for thy nativity, in the day thou wast born thy navel was not cut, neither wast thou washed in water to supple thee; thou wast not salted at all, nor swaddled at all. None eye pitied thee, to do any of these unto thee, to have compassion upon thee; but thou wast cast out in the open field, TO THE LOTHING OF THY PERSON, in the day that thou wast born. And when I passed by thee, and saw thee polluted in thine own blood, I said unto thee when thou wast in thy blood, LIVE;

yea, I said unto thee when thou wast in thy blood, LIVE. I have caused thee to multiply as the bud of the field, and thou hast increased and waxen great, and thou art come to excellent ornaments: thy breasts are fashioned, and thine hair is grown, whereas thou wast naked and bare. *Now* when I passed by thee, and looked upon thee, behold, thy time was the time of love; and I spread my skirt over thee, and covered thy nakedness: yea, I sware unto thee, and entered into a covenant with thee, saith the Lord God, and thou becamest mine. *Then* washed I thee with water; yea, I throughly washed away thy blood from thee, and I anointed thee with oil. I clothed thee also with broidered work, and shod thee with badgers' skin, and I girded thee about with fine linen, and I covered thee with silk. I decked thee also with ornaments, and I put bracelets upon thy hands, and a chain on thy neck. And I put a jewel on thy forehead, and earrings in thine ears, and a beautiful crown upon thine head. Thus wast thou decked with gold and silver; and thy raiment was of fine linen, and silk, and broidered work; thou didst eat fine flour, and honey, and oil: and thou wast exceeding beautiful, and thou didst prosper into a kingdom. And thy renown went forth among the heathen for *thy beauty:* for it was PERFECT THROUGH <u>M-Y</u> COMELINESS, which I had put upon thee, saith the Lord God. *B-u-t* THOU DIDST TRUST IN THINE OWN BEAUTY, and PLAYEDST THE **HARLOT** BECAUSE OF THY RENOWN, and POUREDST OUT THY **FORNICATIONS** ON EVERY ONE THAT PASSED BY; his it was. And of thy garments thou didst take, and deckedst thy high places with divers colours, and playedst the **HARLOT** thereupon: the like things shall not come, neither shall it be so.

Thou hast also taken thy fair jewels of my gold and of my silver, which I had given *thee,* and madest to thyself IMAGES of men, and didst commit **WHOREDOM** with *them,* And tookest thy broidered garments, and coveredst *them:* and thou hast set mine oil and mine incense before *them.* My meat also which I gave *thee,* fine flour, and oil, and honey, wherewith I fed *thee,* thou hast even set it before *them* for a sweet savour: and thus it was, saith the Lord God. M-O-R-E-O-V-E-R THOU HAST TAKEN THY SONS and THY DAUGHTERS, WHOM THOU HAST BORNE UNTO ME, and THESE THAST THOU S-A-C-R-I-F-I-C-E-D UNTO THEM TO BE DEVOURED, IS THIS OF THY **WHOREDOMS** A SMALL MATTER, THAT THOU HAST SLAIN MY CHILDREN, and DELIVERED THEM TO CAUSE THEM TO PASS THROUGH FIRE FOR THEM? *A-n-d* IN ALL THINE ABOMINATIONS and THY **WHOREDOMS** THOU HAST N-O-T REMEMBERED THE DAYS OF THY YOUTH, when thou wast naked and bare, and wast polluted in thy blood. And it came to pass after ALL THY WICKEDNESS, (woe, woe unto thee! saith the Lord God;) That thou hast also built unto thee an EMINENT PLACE, and hast made thee an high place in every street. Thou hast built thy HIGH PLACE at every head of the way, and hast made thy beauty to be abhorred, and hast OPENED THY FEET (LEGS) TO EVERY ONE THAT PASSED BY, and MULTIPLIED THY **WHOREDOMS.** THOU HAST ALSO COMMITTED **FORNICATION** with the Egyptians thy neighbours, great of flesh; and HAST INCREASED THY **WHOREDOME,** TO PROVOKE ME TO ANGER. Behold, therefore I have stretched out my hand over thee, and have diminished thine ordinary food, and delivered thee unto the will of them that H-A-T-E thee, the daughters of the Philistines, which are ashamed of thy lewd way. THOU HASTS PLAYED THE **WHORE** also with the Assyrians, *because* thou wast **u-n-s-a-t-i-a-b-l-e;** yea, THOU HAST PLAYED THE **HARLOT** with them, and yet couldest not be satisfied. Thou hast moreover MULTIPLIED THY **FORNICATION** in the land of Canaan unto Chaldea; and yet thou wast not satisfied therewith. How weak is thine heart, saith the Lord God, seeing thou doest all these things, THE WORK OF AN IMPERIOUS **WHORISH WOMAN;** In that thou buildest thine EMINENT PLACE in the head of every way, and makest thine HIGH PLACE in every street; and hast not been as an **HARLOT,** in that thou scornest hire; *But* AS A WIFE THAT COMMITTETH **ADULTERY,** which taketh strangers instead of her husband! They give gifts to all **WHORES:** but thou givest thy gifts to all thy lovers, and hirest them, that they may come unto thee on every side for thy **WHOREDOM.** *And* the contrary is in thee from other women in thy **WHOREDOMS,** whereas none followeth thee to commit WOREDOMS: and in that thou givest a reward, and no reward is given unto thee, therefore thou art contrary. Wherefore, O **HARLOT,** HEAR THE WORD OF THE LORD: Thus saith the Lord God; *B-e-c-a-u-s-e* THY FILTHINESS WAS POURED OUT, and THY NAKEDNESS DISCOVERED THROUGH THY **WHOREDOMS** WITH THY LOVERS, and WITH ALL THE IDOLS OF THY ABOMINATIONS, and BY THE BLOOD OF THY CHILDREN, WHICH THOU DIDST GIVE UNTO THEM; Behold, therefore I will gather all thy lovers, with whom thou hast taken pleasure, and all them that thou hast loved, with all them that thou hast hated; I WILL EVEN GATHER THEM ROUND ABOUT A-G-A-I-N-S-T THEE, and will discover thy nakedness unto them, that they may see all thy nakedness. *And* I W-I-L-L J-U-D-G-E T-H-E-E, as women that break wedlock and shed blood are judged; and I WILL GIVE THEE BLOOD IN FURY and JEALOUSY. *And* I will **also** give thee into their hand, *and* they shall throw down thine eminent place, *and* shall break down thy high places: they shall strip thee also of thy clothes, *and* shall take thy fair jewels, *and* leave thee naked and bare. They shall **also** bring up a company against thee, *and* they shall stone thee with stones, *and* thrust thee through with their swords. *And* they shall burn thine houses with fire, *and* execute judgments upon thee in the sight of many women: *and* I WILL CAUSE THEE TO C-E-A-S-E FROM PLAYING THE **HARLOT,** and thou also shalt give no hire any more. So will I make MY FURY TOWARD THEE to rest, and MY JEALOUSY shall depart from thee, and I will be quiet, and will be no more angry. *B-e-c-a-u-s-e* thou hast not remembered the days of thy youth, *but* HAST F-R-E-T-T-E-D M-E IN ALL THESE THINGS; behold, *therefore* I ALSO WILL R-E-C-O-M-P-E-N-S-E THY WAY UPON THINE HEAD, saith the Lord God: and thou shalt *not* commit this lewdness above all thine A-B-O-M-I-N-A-T-I-O-N-S. (Ezekiel 16:1-43)

Then I said unto them, What is the HIGH PLACE whereunto ye go? And the name whereof is called Bamah unto this day. Wherefore say unto the house of Israel, Thus saith the Lord GOD; Are ye

64

POLLUTED after the manner of your fathers? and COMMIT YE **WHOREDOM** AFTER THEIR A-B-O-M-I-N-A-T-I-O-N-S? For when ye offer your gifts, when YE MAKE YOUR SONS TO PASS THROUGH THE FIRE, YE POLLUTE YOURSELVES WITH ALL YOUR IDOLS, even unto this day: and shall I be enquired of by you, O house of Israel? As I live, saith the Lord GOD, I WILL NOT BE ENQUIRED OF BY YOU. *And* that which cometh into your mind shall not be at all, that ye say, We will be as the HEATHEN, as the families of the countries, to serve wood and stone. As I live, saith the Lord GOD, surely with a mighty hand, and with a stretched out arm, and with F-U-R-Y POURED OUT, WILL I RULE OVER YOU: And I will bring you out from the people, and will gather you out of the countries wherein ye are scattered, with a mighty hand, and with a stretched out arm, and WITH F-U-R-Y POURED OUT. (Ezekiel 20:29-34)

The word of the Lord came again unto me, saying, Son of man, there were two women, the daughters of one mother: And THEY COMMITTED **WHOREDOMS** in Egypt; they COMMITTED **WHOREDOMS** in their youth: there were their breasts pressed, and there they bruised the teats of their virginity. And the names of them were Aholah the elder, and Aholibah her sister: and THEY WERE MINE, and they bare sons and daughters. Thus were their names; Samaria is Aholah, and Jerusalem Aholibah. And Aholah PLAYED THE **HARLOT** WHEN SHE WAS MINE; and she doted on her lovers, on the Assyrians her neighbours, Which were clothed with blue, captains and rulers, all of them desirable young men, horsemen riding upon horses.  Thus she COMMITTED HER **WHOREDOMS** with them, with all them that were the chosen men of Assyria, and with all on whom she doted: with all their idols she defiled herself.  Neither left she her **WHOREDOMS** brought from Egypt: for in her youth they lay with her, and they bruised the breasts of her virginity, and POURED THEIR **WHOREDOM** UPON HER.  Wherefore I have delivered her into the hand of her lovers, into the hand of the Assyrians, upon whom she doted. These discovered her nakedness: they took her sons and her daughters, and SLEW HER WITH THE SWORD: and she became famous among women; for THEY HAD EXECUTED JUDGMENT UPON HER.  And when her sister Aholibah saw this, she was M-O-R-E CORRUPT in her inordinate love than she, and in her **WHOREDOMS** more than her sister in her **WHOREDOMS.**  She doted upon the Assyrians her neighbours, captains and rulers clothed most gorgeously, horsemen riding upon horses, all of them desirable young men.  Then I saw that she was defiled, that they took both one way,   And that SHE INCREASED HER **WHOREDOMS:** for when she saw men pourtrayed upon the wall, the images of the Chaldeans pourtrayed with vermilion,  Girded with girdles upon their loins, exceeding in dyed attire upon their heads, all of them princes to look to, after the manner of the Babylonians of Chaldea, the land of their nativity:  And as soon as she saw them with her eyes, she doted upon them, and sent messengers unto them into Chaldea.  And the Babylonians came to her into the bed of love, and THEY DEFILED HER WITH THEIR **WHOREDOM,** and she was polluted with them, and her MIND was alienated from them.   So SHE DISCOVERED HER **WHOREDOMS,** and discovered her nakedness: then my mind was alienated from her, like as my mind was alienated from her sister.

*Y-e-t* SHE MULTIPLIED HER **WHOREDOMS,** in calling to remembrance the days of her youth, wherein she had PLAYED THE **HARLOT** in the land of Egypt.  For she doted upon their paramours, whose flesh is as the flesh of asses, and whose issue is like the issue of horses.   Thus thou calledst to remembrance the lewdness of thy youth, in bruising thy teats by the Egyptians for the paps of thy youth. Therefore, O Aholibah, thus saith the Lord God; Behold, I will raise up thy lovers against thee, from whom thy mind is alienated, and I will bring them against thee on every side;   The Babylonians, and all the Chaldeans, Pekod, and Shoa, and Koa, and all the Assyrians with them: all of them desirable young men, captains and rulers, great lords and renowned, all of them riding upon horses.   And THEY SHALL COME AGAINST THEE with chariots, wagons, and wheels, and with an assembly of people, which shall set against thee buckler and shield and helmet round about: and I will set judgment before them, and T-H-E-Y SHALL JUDGE T-H-E-E ACCORDING TO THEIR JUDGMENTS. *And* I WILL SET MY JEALOUSY AGAINST THEE, *and* THEY SHALL DEAL F-U-R-I-O-U-S-L-Y WITH THEE: they shall take away thy nose and thine ears; and thy remnant shall fall by the sword: they shall take thy sons and thy daughters; and thy residue shall be devoured by the fire.   They shall also strip thee out of thy clothes, and take away thy fair jewels.   THUS WILL I MAKE THY LEWDNESS TO CEASE FROM

THEE, and thy **WHOREDOM** brought from the land of Egypt: so that thou shalt not lift up thine eyes unto them, nor remember Egypt any more. For thus saith the Lord God; Behold, I WILL DELIVER THEE INTO THE HAND OF THEM WHOM THOU HATEST, into the hand of them from whom thy mind is alienated: And they shall deal with thee hatefully, and shall take away all thy labour, and shall leave thee naked and bare: and the nakedness of thy **WHOREDOMS** shall be discovered, both thy lewdness and thy **WHOREDOMS.** I will do these things unto thee, *b-e-c-a-u-s-e* thou hast gone a **WHORING** after the heathen, and because thou art polluted with their idols. Thou hast walked in the way of thy sister; therefore will I give her cup into thine hand. Thus saith the Lord God; Thou shalt drink of thy sister's cup deep and large: thou shalt be laughed to scorn and had in derision; it containeth much. Thou shalt be filled with drunkenness and sorrow, with the cup of astonishment and desolation, with the cup of thy sister Samaria. Thou shalt even drink it and suck it out, and thou shalt break the sherds thereof, and pluck off thine own breasts: for I have spoken it, saith the Lord God. Therefore thus saith the Lord God; Because thou hast forgotten me, and cast me behind thy back, therefore bear thou also thy lewdness and thy **WHOREDOMS.** The Lord said moreover unto me; Son of man, wilt thou judge Aholah and Aholibah? yea, declare unto them their abominations; That they have committed **ADULTERY,** and blood is in their hands, and with their idols have they committed **AFULTERY,** and have also caused their sons, whom they bare unto me, to pass for them through the fire, to devour them. Moreover this they have done unto me: they have DEFILED MY SANCTUARY in the same day, and have PROFANED MY SABBATHS. For when they had SLAIN THEIR CHILDREN TO THEIR IDOLS, then they came the same day into my sanctuary to profane it; and, lo, thus have they done in the midst of mine house. And furthermore, that ye have sent for men to come from far, unto whom a messenger was sent; and, lo, they came: for whom thou didst wash thyself, paintedst thy eyes, and deckedst thyself with ornaments, And satest upon a stately bed, and a table prepared before it, whereupon thou hast set mine incense and mine oil. And a voice of a multitude being at ease was with her: and with the men of the common sort were brought Sabeans from the wilderness, which put bracelets upon their hands, and beautiful crowns upon their heads. Then said I unto her that was OLD IN **ADULTERIES,** Will they now commit **WHOREDOMS** with her, and she with them? Yet they went in unto her, as they go in unto a woman that playeth the **HARLOT:** so went they in unto Aholah and unto Aholibah, the lewd women. And the righteous men, they shall judge them after the manner of **ADULTERESSES,** and after the manner of women that shed blood; because they *are* **ADULTERESSES**, and blood is in their hands. For thus saith the Lord God; I will bring up a company upon them, and will give them to be removed and spoiled. And THE COMPANY SHALL STONE THEM WITH STONES, and DISPATCH THEM WITH THEIR SWORDS; THEY SHALL SLAY THEIR SONS and THEIR DAUGHTERS, and BURN UP THEIR HOUSES WITH FIRE. THUS WILL I CAUSE LEWDNESS TO CEASE OUT OF THE LAND, that all women may be taught *not* to do after your lewdness. *And*

THEY SHALL R-E-C-O-M-P-E-N-S-E YOUR LEWDNESS UPON YOU, and ye shall bear the sins of your idols: and ye shall know that I am the Lord God. (Ezekiel 23:1-49)

Afterward he brought me to the gate, even the gate that looketh toward the east: And, behold, the glory of the God of Israel came from the way of the east: and his voice was like a noise of many waters: and the earth shined with his glory. And it was according to the appearance of THE VISION which I saw, even according to THE VISION that I saw when I came to destroy the city: and the visions were like THE VISION that I saw by the river Chebar; and I fell upon my face. And the glory of the LORD came into the house by the way of the gate whose prospect is toward the east. So the spirit took me up, and brought me into the inner court; and, behold, THE GLORY OF THE LORD FILLED THE HOUSE. And I heard him speaking unto me out of the house; and the man stood by me. And he said unto me, Son of man, the place of my throne, and the place of the soles of my feet, where I will dwell in the midst of the children of Israel for ever, and my holy name, shall the house of Israel NO MORE DEFILE, neither they, nor their kings, by their **WHOREDOM,** nor by the carcases of their kings in their high places. In their setting of their threshold by my thresholds, and their post by my posts, and the wall between me and them, THEY HAVE EVEN DEFILED MY HOLY NAME BY THEIR A-B-O-M-I-N-A-T-I-O-N-S THAT THEY HAVE COMMITTED: WHEREFORE I HAVE CONSUMED THEM IN MINE ANGER. Now let them put away their **WHOREDOM,** and the carcases of their kings, far from me, and I will dwell in the midst of them for ever. Thou son of man, shew the house to the house of Israel, THAT THEY MAY BE ASHAMED OF THEIR INIQUITIES: and let them measure the pattern.  And *if* they be ashamed of all that they have done, shew them the form of the house, and the fashion thereof, and the goings out thereof, and the comings in thereof, and all the forms thereof, and all the ordinances thereof, and all the forms thereof, and all the laws thereof: and write it in their sight, THAT THEY MAY KEEP THE W-H-O-L-E FORM THEREOF, *and* A-L-L THE ORDINANCES THEREOF, and "DO" THEM. THIS IS THE L-A-W OF THE HOUSE; Upon the top of the mountain the whole limit thereof round about shall be *most* HOLY. Behold, THIS IS THE L-A-W OF THE HOUSE. (Ezekiel 43:1-12)

Say ye unto your brethren, Ammi; and to your sisters, Ruhamah.  Plead with your mother, PLEAD: for she is not my wife, neither am I her husband: let her therefore put away her **WHOREDOMS** out of her sight, and her **ADULTERIES** from between her breasts;  Lest I strip her naked, and set her as in the day that she was born, and make her as a wilderness, and set her like a dry land, and slay her with thirst.  And I will *not* have mercy upon her children; for they be the CHILDREN OF **WHOREDOMS.**  For their MOTHER HATH PLAYED THE **HARLOT:** she that conceived them hath DONE SHAMEFULLY: for she said, I will go after my lovers, that give me my bread and my water, my wool and my flax, mine oil and my drink. *Therefore,* behold, I will hedge up thy way with thorns, and make a wall, that she shall not find her paths.  And she shall follow after her lovers, but she

71

shall not overtake them; and she shall seek them, but shall not find them: then shall she say, I WILL GO AND RETURN TO MY FIRST HUSBAND; FOR THEN WAS IT BETTER WITH ME THAN NOW. (Hosea 2:1-7)

Then said the LORD unto me, Go yet, love a woman beloved of her friend, yet an **ADULTERESS, according to the love of the LORD toward the children of Israel, who look to other gods, and love flagons of wine.** So I bought her to me for fifteen pieces of silver, and for an homer of barley, and an half homer of barley: And I said unto her, Thou shalt abide for me many days; THOU SHALT NOT PLAY THE **HARLOT,** and thou shalt not be for another man: so will I also be for thee. For the children of Israel shall abide many days without a king, and without a prince, and without a sacrifice, and without an image, and without an ephod, and without teraphim: *Afterward* SHALL THE CHILDREN OF ISRAEL RETURN, and SEEK THE LORD THEIR GOD, and DAVID THEIR KING; and SHALL FEAR THE LORD and HIS GOODNESS IN THE LATTER DAYS. (Hosea 3:1-5)

Hear the word of the Lord, ye children of Israel: for the Lord hath a controversy with the inhabitants of the land, *because* there is NO TRUTH, NOR MERCY, NOR KNOWLEDGE of God in the land. By swearing, and LYING, and KILLING, and STEALING, and COMMITTING **ADULTERY,** they break out, and blood toucheth blood. *Therefore* shall the land mourn, and every one that dwelleth therein shall languish, with the beasts of the field, and with the fowls of heaven; yea, the fishes of the sea also shall be taken away. Yet let no man strive, nor reprove another: for thy people are as they that strive with the priest. *Therefore* SHALT THOU FALL IN THE DAY, and THE PROPHET ALSO SHALL FALL WITH THEE IN THE NIGHT, and I WILL DESTROY THY MOTHER. **MY PEOPLE ARE DESTROYED FOR LACK OF KNOWLEDGE:** *b-e-c-a-u-s-e* THOU HAST REJECTED KNOWLEDGE, I WILL ALSO REJECT THEE, that thou shalt be no priest to me: seeing THOU HAST FORGOTTEN THE LAW OF THY GOD, I WILL ALSO FORGET THY CHILDREN. As they were increased, so they sinned against me: *therefore* WILL I CHANGE THEIR GLORY INTO SHAME. THEY EAT UP THE SIN OF MY PEOPLE, and THEY SET THEIR HEART ON THEIR INIQUITY. And there shall be, like people, like priest: and I WILL PUNISH THEM FOR THEIR WAYS, and REWARD THEM THEIR DOINGS. For they shall eat, and not have enough: they shall commit **WHOREDOM,** and shall not increase: because they have left off to take heed to the Lord. **WHOREDOM** and WINE and NEW WINE TAKE AWAY THE HEART. My people ask counsel at their stocks, and their staff declareth unto them: *for* THE SPIRIT OF **WHOREDOMS** HATH CAUSED THEM TO ERR, and THEY HAVE GONE A **WHORING** FROM UNDER THEIR GOD. They sacrifice upon the tops of the mountains, and burn incense upon the hills, under oaks and poplars and elms, because the shadow thereof is good: therefore your daughters shall commit whoredom, and your spouses shall commit adultery. I will not punish your daughters when they commit **WHOREDOM,** nor your spouses when they commit **ADULTERY:** for themselves are separated with **WHORES**, and they sacrifice with **HARLOTS:** *therefore* THE PEOPLE THAT DOTH NOT UNDERSTAND SHALL FALL. Though thou, Israel, play the **HARLOT,** yet let not Judah offend; and come not ye unto Gilgal, neither go ye up to Bethaven, nor swear, The Lord liveth. For Israel slideth back as a backsliding heifer: now the Lord will feed them as a lamb in a large place. Ephraim is joined to idols: let him alone. Their drink is sour: they have committed **WHOREDOM** C-O-N-T-I-N-U-A-L-L-Y: her rulers with shame do love, Give ye. The wind hath bound her up in her wings, and THEY SHALL BE ASHAMED because of their sacrifices. (Hosea 4:1-19)

Hear ye this, O priests; and hearken, ye house of Israel; and give ye ear, O house of the king; for judgment is toward you, because ye have been a snare on Mizpah, and a net spread upon Tabor. And the revolters are profound to make slaughter, though I have been a rebuker of them all. I know Ephraim, and Israel is not hid from me: for now, O Ephraim, THOU COMMITTEST **WHOREDOM,** and ISRAEL IS DEFILED. They will *not* frame their doings to turn unto their God: for **THE SPIRIT OF WHOREDOMS** is in the midst of them, and THEY HAVE NOT KNOWN THE LORD. And the pride of Israel doth testify to his face: therefore shall Israel and Ephraim FALL IN THEIR INIQUITY: Judah also shall fall with them. They shall go with their flocks and with their herds to seek the LORD; *but* THEY SHALL NOT FIND HIM; H-E H-A-T-H W-I-T-H-D-R-A-W-N H-I-M-S-E-L-F F-R-O-M T-H-E-M. THEY HAVE DEALT TREACHEROUSLY AGAINST THE

LORD: for they have begotten strange children: now shall a <u>month</u> devour them with their portions. (Hosea 5:1-7)

COME, and LET US RETURN UNTO THE LORD: *for* HE HATH T-O-R-N, *and* HE WILL H-E-A-L US; HE HATH S-M-I-T-T-E-N, *and* HE WILL B-I-N-D US UP. After two days will he revive us: in the third day he will raise us up, and we shall live in his sight. Then shall we know, if we follow on to know the LORD: his going forth is prepared as the morning; and he shall come unto us as the rain, as the latter and former rain unto the earth. O Ephraim, what shall I do unto thee? O Judah, what shall I do unto thee? for your *goodness* is as a morning cloud, and as the early dew it goeth away. Therefore have I hewed them by the prophets; I have slain them by the words of my mouth: and thy judgments are as the light that goeth forth. FOR I DESIRED MERCY, and NOT SACRIFICE, and THE KNOWLEDGE OF GOD MORE THAN BURNT OFFERINGS. *B-u-t* THEY LIKE MEN HAVE TRANSGRESSED THE COVENANT: THERE HAVE THEY DEALT TREACHEROUSLY AGAINST ME. Gilead is a city of them that work iniquity, and is polluted with blood. And as troops of robbers wait for a man, so the company of priests murder in the way by consent: for they commit lewdness. I have seen an horrible thing in the house of Israel: there is the **WHOREDOM** of Ephraim, Israel is defiled. Also, O Judah, he hath set an harvest for thee, when I returned the captivity of my people. (Hosea 6:1-11)

When I would have healed Israel, then the iniquity of Ephraim was discovered, and the wickedness of

Samaria: for THEY COMMIT FALSEHOOD; and the thief cometh in, and the troop of robbers spoileth without. And THEY CONSIDER NOT IN THEIR HEARTS THAT -I- R-E-M-E-M-B-E-R A-L-L T-H-E-I-R W-I-C-K-E-D-N-E-S-S: NOW THEIR OWN DOINGS HAVE BESET THEM ABOUT; they are before my face. They make the king glad with their WICKEDNESS, and the princes with their LIES. They are ALL **ADULTERERS,** as an oven heated by the baker, who ceaseth from raising after he hath kneaded the dough, until it be leavened. In the day of our king the princes have made him sick with bottles of wine; he stretched out his hand with scorners. **For they have made ready their *heart* like an oven,** whiles they lie in wait: their baker sleepeth all the night; in the morning it burneth as a flaming fire. They are all hot as an oven, and have devoured their judges; all their kings are fallen: THERE IS NONE AMONG THEM THAT CALLETH UNTO ME. (Hosea 7:1-7)

The word of the LORD that came to Micah the Morasthite in the days of Jotham, Ahaz, and Hezekiah, kings of Judah, which he saw concerning Samaria and Jerusalem. Hear, all ye people; hearken, O earth, and all that therein is: and let the Lord GOD be witness AGAINST you, the LORD from his holy temple. For, behold, the LORD cometh forth out of his place, and will come down, and tread upon the HIGH PLACES of the earth. And the mountains shall be molten under him, and the valleys shall be cleft, as wax before the fire, and as the waters that are poured down a steep place. FOR THE TRANSGRESSION OF JACOB IS ALL THIS, and FOR THE SINS OF THE HOUSE OF

ISRAEL. What is the transgression of Jacob? is it not Samaria? and what are the high places of Judah? are they not Jerusalem? Therefore I will make Samaria as an heap of the field, and as plantings of a vineyard: and I will pour down the stones thereof into the valley, and I will discover the foundations thereof. And ALL THE GRAVEN IMAGES THEREOF SHALL BE BEATEN TO PIECES, and ALL THE HIRES THEREOF SHALL BE BURNED WITH THE FIRE, and ALL THE IDOLS THEREOF SHALL I LAY DESOLATE: FOR SHE GATHERED IT OF THE HIRE OF AN **HARLOT** and THEY SHALL RETURN TO THE HIRE OF AN **HARLOT.** *Therefore* I will wail and howl, I will go stripped and naked: I will make a wailing like the dragons, and mourning as the owls. For her wound is incurable; for it is come unto Judah; he is come unto the gate of my people, even to Jerusalem. (Micah 1:1-9)

WOE to the bloody city! it is all FULL OF LIES and ROBBERY; the prey departeth not; The noise of a whip, and the noise of the rattling of the wheels, and of the pransing horses, and of the jumping chariots. The horseman lifteth up both the bright sword and the glittering spear: and there is A MULTITUDE OF SLAIN, and A GREAT NUMBER OF CARCASES; and THERE IS NONE END OF THEIR CORPSES; they stumble upon their corpses: *B-e-c-a-u-s-e* of the multitude of the **WHOREDOMS** of the wellfavoured **HARLOT,** the MISTRESS OF WITCHCRAFTS, that selleth nations through her **WHOREDOMS,** and families through her WITCHCRAFTS. Behold, -I- A-M A-G-A-I-N-S-T T-H-E-E, saith the LORD of hosts; and I will discover thy skirts upon thy face, and I will shew the nations thy nakedness, and the kingdoms thy shame. *And* I WILL CAST ABOMINABLE FILTH UPON THEE, and MAKE THEE VILE, and will SET THEE AS A GAZINGSTOCK. And it shall come to pass, that all they that look upon thee shall flee from thee, and say, NINEVEH is laid waste: who will bemoan her? whence shall I seek comforters for thee? (Nahum 3:1-7)

*Behold,* I WILL SEND MY MESSENGER, and HE SHALL PREPARE THE WAY BEFORE ME: and the LORD, whom ye seek, shall suddenly come to his temple, even the messenger of the covenant, whom ye delight in: behold, he shall come, saith the LORD of hosts. ***B-u-t*** WHO MAY ABIDE THE DAY OF HIS COMING? and WHO SHALL STAND WHEN HE APPEARETH? FOR HE IS LIKE A <u>REFINER'S F-I-R-E</u>, and LIKE A <u>FULLERS' S-O-A-P</u>: *And* HE SHALL SIT AS A REFINER and PURIFIER OF SILVER: and he shall purify the sons of Levi, and PURGE THEM AS GOLD and SILVER, THAT THEY MAY OFFER UNTO THE LORD AN OFFERING IN RIGHTEOUSNESS. *Then* shall the offering of Judah and Jerusalem be pleasant unto the LORD, as in the days of old, and as in former years. And I WILL COME NEAR TO YOU IN JUDGMENT; and I WILL BE A SWIFT WITNESS AGAINST THE SORCERERS, and AGAINST THE **ADULTERERS,** and AGAINST FALSE SWEARERS, and AGAINST THOSE THAT OPPRESS THE HIRELING IN HIS WAGES, THE WIDOW, and THE FATHERLESS, and THAT TURN ASIDE THE STRANGER FROM HIS RIGHT, and F-E-A-R N-O-T M-E, saith the

LORD of hosts. For I am the LORD, I C-H-A-N-G-E N-O-T; therefore ye sons of Jacob are not consumed. Even from the days of your fathers ye are gone away from mine ordinances, and have not kept them. RETURN UNTO ME, and I WILL RETURN UNTO YOU, saith the LORD of hosts. But ye said, Wherein shall we return? WILL A MAN ROB GOD? Y-E-T Y-E H-A-V-E R-O-B-B-E-D M-E. But ye say, Wherein have we robbed thee? I-N T-I-T-H-E-S *a-n-d* O-F-F-E-R-I-N-G-S. YE ARE CURSED WITH A CURSE: FOR YE HAVE ROBBED ME, even this whole nation. Bring ye all the tithes into the storehouse, that there may be meat in mine house, and prove me now herewith, saith the LORD of hosts, if I will not open you the windows of heaven, and pour you out a blessing, that there shall not be room enough to receive it. And I will rebuke the devourer for your sakes, and he shall not destroy the fruits of your ground; neither shall your vine cast her fruit before the time in the field, saith the LORD of hosts. And all nations shall call you BLESSED: for ye shall be a delightsome land, saith the LORD of hosts. YOUR WORDS HAVE BEEN STOUT AGAINST ME, saith the LORD. Yet ye say, WHAT HAVE WE SPOKEN SO MUCH AGAINST THEE? Ye have said, IT IS VAIN TO SERVE GOD: and WHAT PROFIT IS IT THAT WE HAVE KEPT HIS ORDINANCE, and THAT WE HAVE WALKED MOURNFULLY BEFORE THE LORD OF HOSTS? And now we call the PROUD happy; yea, they that work WICKEDNESS are set up; yea, they that TEMPT GOD are even delivered.

# THEN THEY THAT FEARED THE LORD SPAKE OFTEN ONE TO ANOTHER:

*and*

# THE LORD HEARKENED,

*and*

# HEARD IT,

*and*

# "A BOOK OF REMEMBRANCE"

# WAS WRITTEN BEFORE THEM THAT FEARED THE LORD,

# *and*

# THAT THOUGHT UPON HIS NAME.

*And they shall be mine, saith the LORD of hosts, in that day when I make up my jewels; and I will spare them, as a man spareth his own son that serveth him.* **T-h-e-n** SHALL YE RETURN, and DISCERN BETWEEN THE RIGHTEOUS and THE WICKED, BETWEEN HIM THAT SERVETH GOD and HIM THAT SERVETH HIM NOT. (Malachi 3:1-18)

# SPIRITUAL

## NEW TESTAMENT

But he answered and said unto them, An <u>EVIL</u> and **ADULTEROUS** generation seeketh after a sign; and there shall no sign be given to it, *but* <u>the sign of the prophet Jonas</u>: (Matthew 12:39)

A <u>WICKED</u> and **ADULTEROUS** generation seeketh after a sign; and there shall no sign be given unto it, but the sign of the prophet Jonas. And he left them, and departed. (Matthew 16:4)

And when he had called the people unto him with his disciples also, he said unto them, WHOSOEVER WILL COME AFTER ME, LET HIM (1) <u>DENY HIMSELF</u> (DENY HIS OWN ENTICEMENT TO SIN), and (2) <u>TAKE UP HIS CROSS</u> ("NAIL" SIN; REFUSE THE TEMPATION TO SIN), and (3) <u>FOLLOW ME</u> (FOLLOW MY EXAMPLE OF SINLESS LIVING). For whosoever will SAVE HIS LIFE (SPARE YOURSELF TO RESIST SIN) **shall lose it (eternally);** *but* whosoever shall LOSE HIS LIFE (FORFEIT, REFUSE THE PLEASURES OF SIN) for my sake and the gospel's, the same **shall save it (eternally).** FOR WHAT SHALL IT PROFIT A MAN, IF HE SHALL GAIN THE WHOLE WORLD, and LOSE HIS OWN SOUL? OR WHAT SHALL A MAN GIVE IN EXCHANGE FOR HIS SOUL? WHOSOEVER THEREFORE

SHALL BE ASHAMED OF ME AND OF MY WORDS IN THIS **ADULTEROUS** and SINFUL GENERATION; OF HIM ALSO SHALL THE SON OF MAN BE ASHAMED, when he cometh in the glory of his Father with the holy angels. (Mark 8:34-38)

Jesus answered them, **Verily, verily,** I say unto you, WHOSOEVER COMMITTETH SIN IS THE SERVANT OF SIN. And the servant abideth not in the house for ever: but the Son abideth ever. *If the Son therefore shall make you free, ye shall be free indeed.* I know that ye are Abraham's seed; but ye seek to kill me, *b-e-c-a-u-s-e* my word hath no place in you. I speak that which I have seen with *my* Father: and ye do that which ye have seen with *your* father. They answered and said unto him, Abraham is our father. Jesus saith unto them, *If* ye were Abraham's (spiritual) children, ye would DO the works of Abraham. *But* NOW YE SEEK TO KILL ME, A MAN THAT HATH TOLD YOU THE TRUTH, which I have heard of God: this did not Abraham. Ye DO the deeds of your father. Then said they to him, We be not born of (spiritual) **FORNICATION;** we have one Father, even God. Jesus said unto them, *If* God were your Father, YE WOULD LOVE ME: for I proceeded forth and came from God; neither came I of myself, but he sent me. Why do ye *not* understand my speech? even *b-e-c-a-u-s-e* YE CANNOT HEAR (UNDERSTAND) MY WORD. YE ARE OF YOUR FATHER THE DEVIL, and THE LUSTS OF YOUR FATHER YE WILL DO. HE WAS A M-U-R-D-E-R-E-R FROM THE BEGINNING, and ABODE N-O-T IN THE TRUTH, *because* THERE IS N-O-T TRUTH IN HIM. WHEN HE

84

SPEAKETH A L-I-E, HE SPEAKETH OF HIS OWN: for HE IS A L-I-A-R, and THE F-A-T-H-E-R OF IT. *And* BECAUSE I TELL YOU THE TRUTH, YE BELIEVE ME NOT. Which of you convinceth me of sin? And if I say the truth, why do ye not believe me? HE THAT IS OF GOD HEARETH GOD'S WORDS: **ye therefore hear them *not*, because ye are *not* of God.** Then answered the Jews, and said unto him, Say we not well that thou art a Samaritan, and hast a devil? Jesus answered, I have N-O-T a devil; but I honour my Father, and <u>ye do dishonour me</u>. And I SEEK N-O-T MINE OWN GLORY: there is one that seeketh and judgeth. *Verily, verily, I say unto you, If a man keep my saying, he shall never see death.* Then said the Jews unto him, <u>Now we know that thou hast a devil</u>. Abraham is dead, and the prophets; and thou sayest, If a man keep my saying, he shall never taste of death. Art thou greater than our father Abraham, which is dead? and the prophets are dead: whom makest thou thyself? Jesus answered, If I honour myself, my honour is nothing: it is my Father that honoureth me; of whom ye say, that he is your God: Yet ye have not known him; but I know him: and if I should say, I know him not, I shall be a liar like unto you: but I KNOW HIM, and (because I) KEEP HIS SAYING. (John 8:34-55)

Moreover, brethren, I would not that ye should be ignorant, how that all our fathers were under the cloud, and all passed through the sea; And were all baptized unto Moses in the cloud and in the sea; And did all eat the same spiritual meat; And did all drink the same spiritual drink: for they drank of that spiritual Rock that followed them: and that Rock was Christ. *But* **with many of them God was not well pleased: for they were OVERTHROWN in the wilderness.** Now these things were our EXAMPLES, to the intent WE SHOULD N-O-T LUST AFTER EVIL THINGS, as they also lusted. *Neither* be ye IDOLATERS, as were some of them; as it is written, The people sat down to eat and drink, and rose up to play. NEITHER LET US COMMIT **FORNICATION,** as some of them committed, and **fell** in one day three and twenty thousand (23,000). *Neither* let is TEMPT CHRIST, as some of them also tempted, and were **destroyed of serpents**. *Neither* MURMER ye, as some of them also murmured, and were **destroyed of the destroyer.** Now all these things happened unto them for EXAMPLES: and they are written for our ADMONITION, upon whom the ends of the world are come. Wherefore let him that thinketh he standeth TAKE HEED lest he fall. There hath no temptation taken you but such as is common to man: *b-u-t God is faithful, who will not suffer you to be tempted above that ye are able; but will with the temptation also make a way to escape, that ye may be able to bear it.* Wherefore, my dearly beloved, FLEE FROM IDOLATRY. (1 Corinthians 10:1-14)

Looking D-I-L-I-G-E-N-T-L-Y lest any man fail of the grace of God; lest any root of bitterness springing up trouble you, and thereby many be defiled; Lest there be any **FORNICATOR,** or PROFANE PERSON, as Esau, who for one morsel of meat sold his birthright. For ye know how that afterward, when he would have inherited the blessing, he was R-E-J-E-C-T-E-D: for he found

NO PLACE OF REPENTANCE, though he sought it carefully with tears. (Hebrews 12:15-17)

And to the angel of the church in <u>Pergamos</u> write; *These things saith he (Jesus) which hath the sharp sword with two edges;* <u>I know thy works, and where thou dwellest, even where Satan's seat is: and thou holdest fast my name, and hast not denied my faith, even in those days wherein Antipas was my faithful martyr, who was slain among you, where Satan dwelleth.</u> ***B-u-t*** I HAVE A FEW THINGS AGAINST THEE, because thou hast there them that hold THE DOCTRINE OF BALAAM, who taught Balac to cast a <u>stumblingblock before</u> the children of Israel, <u>to eat things sacrificed unto idols,</u> and to commit **FORNICATION.** So hast thou also them that hold the DOCTRINE OF THE NICOLAITANES (GENERALLY, A SELF INDULGENT LIFESTYLE, ESPECIALLY SEXUALLY, AND EATING FOOD SACRIFICED TO IDOLS) AND, WHICH THING -I- H-A-T-E. R-E-P-E-N-T; *or else* <u>I will come unto thee quickly, and will fight against them with the sword of my mouth.</u> *He that hath an ear, let him hear what the Spirit saith unto the churches;* To him that O-V-E-R-C-O-M-E-T-H will I give to eat of the <u>hidden manna,</u> and will give him a <u>white stone,</u> and in the stone a <u>new name</u> written, which no man knoweth saving he that receiveth it. And unto the angel of the church in <u>Thyatira</u> write; *These things saith the Son of God, who hath his eyes like unto a flame of fire, and his feet are like fine brass;* I know thy <u>works,</u> and <u>charity,</u> and <u>service,</u> and <u>faith,</u> and thy <u>patience,</u> and thy <u>works</u>; and the last to be more than the first. ***N-o-t-w-i-t-h-s-t-a-n-d-i-n-g*** I HAVE A FEW THINGS AGAINST THEE, *because* <u>thou</u>

sufferest that woman Jezebel, which calleth herself a prophetess, to teach and to seduce my servants to commit **FORNICATION,** *and* TO EAT THINGS SACRIFICED UNTO IDOLS. And I gave her space to repent of her **FORNICATION;** *a-n-d (b-u-t)* she repented NOT. **Behold, I will cast her into a bed,** *and* **them that commit ADULTERY with her into g-r-e-a-t       t-r-i-b-u-l-a-t-i-o-n,** *except* **they repent of their deeds.** *And* I WILL KILL HER CHILDREN WITH DEATH; and all the churches shall know that (...............)

# I AM HE WHICH

# S-E-A-R-C-H-E-T-H

# *the* REINS

# *and* HEARTS:

# *and*

# I WILL GIVE UNTO EVERY ONE OF YOU ACCORDING TO YOUR W-O-R-K-S.

But unto you I say, and unto the rest in Thyatira, as many as have *not* this doctrine, and which have *not* known the depths of Satan, as they speak; *I will put upon you none other burden.* But that which ye have already HOLD FAST TILL I COME. And he that O-V-E-R-C-O-M-E-T-H, *and* KEEPETH MY WORKS UNTO THE END, *to him will I give power over the nations:* And he shall rule them with a rod of iron; as the vessels of a potter shall they be broken to shivers: even as I received of my Father. And I will give him the morning star. HE THAT HATH AN EAR, LET HIM HEAR WHAT THE SPIRIT SAITH UNTO THE CHURCHES. (Revelation 2:12-29)

And I saw *another* angel fly in the midst of heaven, having the EVERLASTING GOSPEL to preach unto them that dwell on the earth, and to every nation, and kindred, and tongue, and people, Saying with a loud voice, FEAR GOD, and GIVE GLORY TO HIM; FOR THE HOUR OF HIS JUDGMENT IS COME: and WORSHIP HIM that made heaven, and earth, and the sea, and the fountains of waters. And there followed another angel, saying, **Babylon is fallen, is fallen, that great city, *b-e-c-a-u-s-e* she made all nations drink of the wine of the wrath of her FORNICATION.** And the third angel followed them, saying with a loud voice, IF ANY MAN WORSHIP THE BEAST and HIS IMAGE, and RECEIVE HIS MARK IN HIS FOREHEAD, or IN HIS HAND, THE SAME SHALL DRINK OF THE WINE OF THE WRATH OF GOD, WHICH IS POURED OUT WITHOUT MIXTURE INTO THE CUP OF HIS INDIGNATION; and HE SHALL BE T-O-R-M-E-N-T-E-D WITH FIRE and

BRIMSTONE IN THE PRESENCE OF THE HOLY ANGELS, *and* IN THE PRESENCE OF THE LAMB: And the smoke of their torment ascendeth up for ever and ever: *and* THEY HAVE N-O  R-E-S-T DAY NOR NIGHT, WHO WORSHIP THE BEAST and HIS IMAGE, *and* WHOSOEVER RECEIVETH THE MARK OF HIS NAME. (Revelation 14:6-11)

And there came one of the SEVEN ANGELS which had the SEVEN VIALS, and talked with me, saying unto me, Come hither; I will shew unto thee THE JUDGMENT OF THE GREAT **WHORE** that sitteth upon many waters: With whom THE KINGS OF THE EARTH have committed **FORNICATION,** and the inhabitants of the earth have been made drunk with the wine of her **FORNICATION.** So he carried me away in the spirit into the wilderness: and I SAW A WOMAN SIT UPON A SCARLET COLOURED BEAST, full of names of blasphemy, having seven heads and ten horns. And THE WOMAN was arrayed in purple and scarlet colour, and decked with gold and precious stones and pearls, having a golden cup in her hand full of abominations and FILTHINESS OF HER **FORNICATION:** And upon her forehead was a name written, MYSTERY, BABYLON THE GREAT, THE MOTHER OF **HARLOTS** AND ABOMINATIONS OF THE EARTH. And I saw the woman drunken with the blood of the saints, and with the blood of the MARTYRS of Jesus: and when I saw her, I wondered with great admiration. And the angel said unto me, Wherefore didst thou marvel? I will tell thee the mystery of the woman, and of the beast that carrieth her, which hath the seven heads and ten horns. The beast that thou sawest was, and is not; and shall ascend out of the bottomless pit, and go into perdition: and they that dwell on the earth shall wonder, whose names were **NOT** written in the BOOK OF LIFE from the foundation of the world, when they behold the beast that <u>was</u>, and <u>is not</u>, and <u>yet is</u>. (Revelation 17:1-8)

And after these things I saw another angel come down from heaven, having great power; and the earth was lightened with his glory. And he cried mightily with a strong voice, saying, BABYLON THE GREAT IS FALLEN, IS FALLEN, and IS BECOME THE HABITATION OF DEVILS, and THE HOLD OF EVERY FOUL SPIRIT, and A CAGE OF EVERY UNCLEAN AND HATEFUL BIRD. FOR ALL NATIONS HAVE DRUNK OF THE WINE OF THE WRATH OF HER **FORNICATION,** and THE KINGS OF THE EARTH HAVE COMMITTED **FORNICATION** WITH HER, and the merchants of the earth are waxed rich through the abundance of her delicacies. And I heard another voice from heaven, saying, COME OUT OF HER, MY PEOPLE, THAT YE BE NOT PARTAKERS OF HER SINS, and THAT YE RECEIVE NOT OF HER PLAGUES. FOR HER SINS HAVE REACHED UNTO HEAVEN, and GOD HATH REMEMBERED HER INIQUITIES. REWARD HER EVEN AS SHE REWARDED YOU, and D-O-U-B-L-E UNTO HER D-O-U-B-L-E ACCORDING TO HER WORKS: IN THE CUP WHICH SHE HATH FILLED FILL TO HER D-O-U-B-L-E. How much she hath glorified herself, and lived deliciously, SO MUCH T-O-R-M-E-N-T and S-O-R-R-O-W GIVE HER: for she saith in her heart, I sit a queen, and am no widow, and shall see no sorrow. Therefore shall her plagues come in one day, death, and mourning, and famine; and she shall be utterly burned with fire: for strong is the Lord God who judgeth her. And THE KINGS OF THE EARTH, WHO HAVE COMMITTED **FORNICATION** and LIVED DELICIOUSLY WITH HER, SHALL BEWAIL HER, and LAMENT FOR HER, WHEN THEY SHALL SEE THE SMOKE OF HER B-U-R-N-I-N-G, Standing afar off for the fear of her torment, saying, ALAS, ALAS THAT GREAT CITY BABYLON, THAT MIGHTY CITY! FOR IN ONE HOUR IS THY JUDGMENT COME. (Revelation 18:1-10)

*And after these things I heard a great voice of much people in heaven, saying, Alleluia; Salvation, and glory, and honour, and power, unto the Lord our God: For true and righteous are his judgments:* for HE HATH JUDGED THE GREAT **WHORE,** WHICH DID CORRUPT THE EARTH WITH HER **FORNICATION,** and HATH AVENGED THE BLOOD OF HIS SERVANTS AT HER HAND. And again they said, Alleluia And her smoke rose up for ever and ever. (Revelation 19:1-3)

# FROWARD

THEY PROVOKE HIM TO JEALOUSY WITH
STRANGE GODS, WITH ABOMINATIONS
PROVOKE THEY HIM TO ANGER. They
sacrificed unto devils, not to God; to gods whom
they knew not, to new gods that came newly up,
whom your fathers feared not. OF THE ROCK
THAT BEGAT THEE THOU ART UNMINDFUL,
and HAST FORGOTTEN GOD THAT FORMED
THEE. And when the LORD saw it, H-E A-B-H-O-R-
R-E-D T-H-E-M, because of the provoking of his
sons, and of his daughters. And he said, **I will hide
my face from them, I will see what their end
shall be: for they are a v-e-r-y FROWARD
generation, children in whom is no faith.** THEY
HAVE MOVED ME TO JEALOUSY with that
which is not God; THEY HAVE PROVOKED ME
TO ANGER with their vanities: and **I will move**
*them* **to jealousy** with those which are not a people;
**I will provoke** *them* **to anger** with a foolish nation.
**FOR A FIRE IS KINDLED IN MINE ANGER,
and SHALL BURN UNTO THE L-O-W-E-S-T
H-E-L-L,** and shall consume the earth with her
increase, and set on fire the foundations of the
mountains. I will heap mischiefs upon them; I will
spend mine arrows upon them. They shall be burnt
with hunger, and devoured with burning heat, and
with bitter destruction: I will also send the teeth of
beasts upon them, with the poison of serpents of the
dust. The sword without, and terror within, shall
destroy both the young man and the virgin, the

suckling also with the man of gray hairs. (Deuteronomy 32:16-25)

*The LORD rewarded me according to my righteousness: according to the cleanness of my hands hath he recompensed me. For I have kept the ways of the LORD, and have not wickedly departed from my God. For all his judgments were before me: and as for his statutes, I did not depart from them. I was also upright before him, and have kept myself from mine iniquity. Therefore the LORD hath recompensed me according to my righteousness; according to my cleanness in his eye sight.* With the MERCIFUL thou wilt shew thyself MERCIFUL, and with the UPRIGHT man thou wilt shew thyself UPRIGHT. With the PURE thou wilt shew thyself PURE; and with the **FROWARD** thou wilt shew thyself UNSAVOURY. And the AFFLICTED people thou wilt SAVE: *but* thine eyes are upon the HAUGHTY, that thou mayest BRING THEM DOWN. For thou art my lamp, O LORD: and the LORD will lighten my darkness. (2 Samuel 22:21-29)

Although affliction cometh *not* forth of the dust, *neither* doth trouble spring out of the ground; *Y-e-t* MAN IS BORN UNTO TROUBLE, as the sparks fly upward. I would seek unto God, and unto God would I commit my cause: Which doeth great things and unsearchable; marvellous things without number: Who giveth rain upon the earth, and sendeth waters upon the fields: To set up on high those that be low; that those which mourn may be exalted to safety. He disappointeth the devices of the CRAFTY, so that their hands cannot perform their enterprise. He taketh the wise in their own

CRAFTINESS: and the counsel of the **FROWARD** is carried headlong. They meet with darkness in the day time, and grope in the noonday as in the night. *B-u-t* he saveth the POOR from the sword, from their mouth, and from the hand of the mighty. *So the poor hath hope, and iniquity stoppeth her mouth.* BEHOLD, HAPPY IS THE MAN WHOM GOD C-O-R-R-E-C-T-E-T-H: *therefore* DESPISE NOT THOU THE C-H-A-S-T-E-N-I-N-G OF THE ALMIGHT: FOR HE MAKETH S-O-R-E, *and* BINDETH UP: HE W-O-U-N-D-E-T-H, and HIS HANDS MAKE WHOLE. (Job 5:6-18)

*The LORD rewarded me according to my righteousness; according to the cleanness of my hands hath he r-e-c-o-m-p-e-n-s-e-d me.* **For** *I have kept the ways of the LORD, and have not wickedly departed from my God. For all his judgments were before me, and I did not put away his statutes from me. I was also upright before him, and I kept myself from mine iniquity. Therefore hath the LORD recompensed me according to my righteousness, according to the cleanness of my hands in his eyesight.* With the MERCIFUL thou wilt shew thyself MERCIFUL; with an UPRIGHT man thou wilt shew thyself UPRIGHT; With the PURE thou wilt shew thyself PURE; *and* **with the FROWARD thou wilt shew thyself FROWARD.** For thou wilt save the afflicted people; but wilt bring down high looks. (Psalm 18:20-27)

I will sing of mercy and judgment: unto thee, O LORD, will I sing. I WILL BEHAVE MYSELF WISELY IN A PERFECT WAY. O when wilt thou come unto me? I will walk within my house with a P-E-R-F-E-C-T H-E-A-R-T. I will set no wicked thing before mine eyes: I H-A-T-E the work of them that TURN ASIDE; it shall not cleave to me. A **FROWARD** heart shall depart from me**: I will *not* know a <u>wicked person</u>.** Whoso PRIVILY SLANDERETH HIS NEIGHBOUR, him will I "cut off:" him that hath an HIGH LOOK and a PROUD HEART will not I suffer. *Mine eyes shall be upon the faithful of the land, that they may dwell with me: he that walketh in a perfect way, he shall serve me.* He that worketh DECEIT shall *not* dwell within my house: he that telleth LIES shall *not* tarry in my sight. I will early DESTROY ALL THE WICKED of the land; that I may "cut off" all wicked doers from the city of the LORD. (Psalm 101:1-8)

*For the LORD giveth wisdom: out of his mouth cometh knowledge and understanding. He layeth up sound wisdom for the righteous: he is a buckler to them that walk uprightly. He keepeth the paths of judgment, and preserveth the way of his saints. Then shalt thou understand righteousness, and judgment, and equity; yea, every good path. When wisdom entereth into thine heart, and knowledge is pleasant unto thy soul; Discretion shall preserve thee, understanding shall keep thee:* To deliver thee from the way of the EVIL MAN, from the man that speaketh **FROWARD** things; **Who <u>leave</u> the paths of uprightness,** to WALK IN THE WAYS OF DARKNESS; Who REJOICE TO DO EVIL, and DELIGHT IN THE **FROWARDNESS** OF THE WICKED; WHOSE WAYS ARE CROOKED, and THEY **FROWARD** IN THEIR PATHS: (Proverbs 2:6-15)

Withhold *not* good from them to whom it is due, when it is in the power of thine hand to do it. Say *not* unto thy neighbour, Go, and come again, and to morrow I will give; when thou hast it by thee. Devise *not* evil against thy neighbour, seeing he dwelleth securely by thee. Strive *not* with a man without cause, if he have done thee no harm. Envy thou *not* the oppressor, and choose **n-o-n-e** of his ways. For the **FOWARD** IS A-B-O-M-I-N-A-T-I-O-N to the LORD: *but **his secret is with the righteous**.* THE C-U-R-S-E OF THE LORD IS IN THE HOUSE OF THE WICKED: *but he blesseth the habitation of the just.* Surely he SCORNETH the SCORNERS: *but he giveth grace unto the lowly.* The wise shall inherit glory: *but* SHAME SHALL BE THE PROMOTION OF THE F-O-O-L-S. (Proverbs 3:27-35)

*My son, attend to my words; incline thine ear unto my sayings. Let them not depart from thine eyes; keep them in the midst of thine heart. For they are life unto those that find them, and health to all their flesh. Keep thy HEART with all diligence; for out of it are the issues of life.* PUT AWAY FROM THEE A **FROWARD** MOUTH, and PERVERSE LIPS PUT FAR FROM THEE. Let thine eyes look right on, and let thine eyelids look straight before thee. Ponder the path of thy feet, and let all thy ways be established. TURN NOT TO THE RIGHT HAND NOR TO THE LEFT: remove thy foot from evil. (Proverbs 4:20-27)

A NAUGHTY person, a WICKED man, walketh with a **FROWARD** M-O-U-T-H. He winketh with his eyes, he speaketh with his feet, he teacheth with his fingers; **FROWARDNESS** IS IN HIS H-E-A-R-T, HE DEVISETH MISCHIEF C-O-N-T-I-N-U-A-L-L-Y; HE SOWETH DISCORD. **Therefore shall his** calamity come *s-u-d-d-e-n-l-y;*  *s-u-d-d-e-n-l-y* **shall he be broken without remedy.** These SIX things doth the LORD H-A-T-E: yea, SEVEN are an A-B-O-M-I-N-A-T-I-O-N unto him:  **(1) <u>A proud look</u>, (2) <u>a lying tongue</u>, and (3) <u>hands that shed innocent blood</u>,  (4) <u>An heart that deviseth wicked imaginations</u>, (5) <u>feet that be swift in running to mischief</u>,  (6) <u>A false witness that speaketh lies</u>,** *and* **(7) <u>he that soweth discord among brethren</u>.** My son, keep thy father's C-O-M-M-A-N-D-M-E-N-T, and forsake not the L-A-W of thy mother:  Bind them continually upon thine HEART, and tie them about thy NECK.  When thou *goest,* it shall lead thee; when thou *sleepest,* it shall keep thee; and when thou *awakest,* it shall talk with thee.  For the C-O-M-M-A-N-D-M-E-N-T  is a lamp; and the L-A-W is light; and <u>REPROOFS of instruction are the way of life</u>:  (Proverbs 6:12-23)

O ye simple, understand WISDOM: and, YE F-O-O-L-S, be ye of an understanding heart.  Hear; for I (WISDOM) will speak of *excellent* things; and the opening of my lips shall be *right* things.  For my mouth shall speak *truth;* and WICKEDNESS is an A-B-O-M-I-N-A-T-I-O-N to my lips.  All the words of my mouth are in *righteousness;* there is N-O-T-H-I-N-G **FROWARD** or PERVERSE in them.  They are all *plain* to him that understandeth, and *right* to them that find knowledge.  Receive my instruction, and not silver; and knowledge rather than choice gold.  For WISDOM is better than rubies; and all the things that may be desired are *not* to be compared to it.  I WISDOM dwell with *prudence,* and find out knowledge of witty inventions.  THE FEAR OF THE LORD IS TO H-A-T-E EVIL:  PRIDE, and ARROGANCY, and

THE EVIL WAY, and THE **FROWARD** MOUTH, DO I H-A-T-E. Counsel is mine, and sound wisdom: I am *understanding;* I have *strength.* (Proverbs 8:5-14)

*The fear of the L*ORD *prolongeth days: b-u-t* THE YEARS OF THE WICKED SHALL BE SHORTENED. *The hope of the righteous shall be gladness: b-u-t* THE EXPECTATION OF THE WICKED SHALL PERISH. *The way of the L*ORD *is strength to the upright: b-u-t* DESTRUCTION SHALL BE TO THE WORKERS OF INIQUITY. *The righteous shall never be removed: b-u-t* THE WICKED SHALL NOT INHABIT THE EARTH. *The mouth of the just bringeth forth wisdom: b-u-t* THE FROWARD TONGUE SHALL BE CUT OUT. *The lips of the righteous know what is acceptable:* ***b-u-t*** THE MOUTH OF THE WICKED SPEAKETH **FROWARDNESS.** (Proverbs 10:27-32)

*The merciful man doeth good to his own soul: b-u-t* HE THAT IS CRUEL TROUBLETH HIS OWN FLESH. THE WICKED WORKETH A DECEITFUL WORK: *b-u-t to him that soweth righteousness shall be a sure reward. As righteousness tendeth to life:* SO HE THAT PURSUETH EVIL PURSUETH IT TO HIS OWN DEATH. THEY THAT ARE OF A **FROWARD** HEART ARE A-B-O-M-I-N-A-T-I-O-N TO THE LORD: *b-u-t such as are upright in their way are his delight.* Though hand join in hand, THE WICKED SHALL N-O-T BE UNPUNISHED: *b-u-t the seed of the righteous shall be delivered.* (Proverbs 11:17-21)

AN UNGODLY MAN DIGGETH UP EVIL: *and* IN HIS LIPS THERE IS AS A BURNING FIRE. A **FROWARD** MAN SOWETH STRIFE: *and* A WHISPERER SEPARATETH CHIEF FRIENDS. A VIOLENT MAN ENTICETH HIS NEIGHBOUR, *and* LEADETH HIM INTO THE WAY THAT IS N-O-T GOOD. HE SHUTTETH HIS EYES TO DEVISE **FROWARD** THINGS: MOVING HIS LIPS HE BRINGETH EVIL TO PASS. (Proverbs 16:27-30)

A MAN VOID OF UNDERSTANDING STRIKETH HANDS, and BECOMETH SURETY IN THE PRESENCE OF HIS FRIEND. HE LOVETH TRANSGESSION THAT LOVETH STRIFE: and HE THAT EXALTETH HIS GATE SEEKETH DESTRUCTION. HE THAT HATH A **FROWARD** HEART FINDETH NO GOOD: and HE THAT HATH A PERVERSE TONGUE FALLETH INTO MISCHIEF. HE THAT BEGETTETH A FOOL DOETH IT TO HIS SORRW: and THE FATHER OF A FOOL HATH NO JOY. (Proverbs 17:18-21)

Every way of a man is right in his own eyes: *b-u-t* THE LORD PONDERETH THE H-E-A-R-T-S. *To do justice and judgment is more acceptable to the LORD than sacrifice.* AN HIGH LOOK, and A PROUD HEART, and THE PLOWING OF THE WICKED, IS SIN. *The thoughts of the diligent tend only to plenteousness; b-u-t* OF EVERY ONE THAT IS HASTY ONLY TO WANT. THE GETTING OF TREASURES BY A LYING TONGUE IS A VANITY TOSSED TO AND FRO OF THEM THAT SEEK DEATH. THE ROBBERY OF THE WICKED SHALL DESTROY

THEM; *b-e-c-a-u-s-e* THEY R-E-F-U-S-E TO DO JUDGMENT. THE WAY OF MAN IS **FROWARD** and STRANGE: *b-u-t as for the pure, his work is right.* (Proverbs 21:2-8)

THORNS and SNARES ARE IN THE WAY OF THE **FROWARD:** *he that doth keep his soul shall be far from them.* (Proverbs 22:5)

For thus saith the high and lofty One that inhabiteth eternity, whose name is Holy; *I dwell in the high and holy place, with him also that is of a contrite and humble spirit, to revive the spirit of the humble, and to revive the heart of the contrite ones.* **For I will not contend for ever, neither will I be always wroth:** for the spirit should fail before me, and the souls which I have made. FOR THE INIQUITY OF HIS COVETOUSNESS WAS I WROTH, and SMOTE HIM: I HID ME, and WAS WROTH, and HE WENT ON **FROWARDLY** IN THE WAY OF HIS H-E-A-R-T. I have seen his ways, and will heal him: I will lead him also, and restore comforts unto him and to his mourners. I create the fruit of the lips; Peace, peace to him that is far off, and to him that is near, saith the LORD; and I will heal him. *B-u-t* THE WICKED ARE LIKE THE TROUBLED SEA, WHEN IT CANNOT REST, whose waters cast up mire and dirt. THERE IS NO PEACE, saith my God, TO THE WICKED. (Isaiah 57:15-21)

As free, and ***not*** USING YOUR LIBERTY FOR A CLOKE OF MALICIOUSNESS, *but* as the *servants of God.* Honour all men. Love the brotherhood. Fear God. Honour the king. Servants, be subject to your masters with all fear; not only to the good and gentle, *but* ALSO TO THE **FROWARD.** For this is thankworthy, if a man for conscience toward God **endure grief, suffering wrongfully.** For what glory is it, if, when ye be buffeted for your faults, ye shall take it patiently? *but if,* WHEN YE DO WELL, and SUFFER FOR IT, YE TAKE IT PATIENTLY, THIS IS ACCEPTABLE WITH GOD. **For even hereunto were ye called:** *b-e-c-a-u-s-e* CHRIST ALSO SUFFERED FOR US, LEAVING US AN EXAMPLE, THAT YE SHOULD FOLLOW HIS STEPS: Who did no sin, neither was guile found in his mouth: **Who, when he was reviled, reviled not again; when he suffered, he threatened not;** *b-u-t committed himself to him that judgeth righteously:* Who his own self bare our sins in his own body on the tree, that WE, being DEAD TO SINS, *should live unto righteousness:* by whose stripes ye were healed. For ye were as sheep going astray; but are now returned unto the Shepherd and Bishop of your souls. (1 Peter 2:16-25)

# FOOL

## (Psalms, Proverbs & N.T.)

Give ear to my words, O LORD, consider my meditation. Hearken unto the voice of my cry, my King, and my God: for UNTO THEE WILL I PRAY. *My voice shalt thou hear in the morning, O LORD; in the morning will I direct my prayer unto thee, and will look up.* For thou art **not** a God that hath pleasure in WICKEDNESS: neither shall EVIL dwell with thee. THE **FOOLISH** SHALL NOT STAND IN THY SIGHT: THOU H-A-T-E-S-T ALL WORKERS OF INIQUITY. Thou shalt **d-e-s-t-r-o-y** them that speak LEASING (LIES): the LORD will A-B-H-O-R the BLOODY and DECEITFUL man. *But* as for me, I will come into thy house in the multitude of thy mercy: and in thy fear will I worship toward thy holy temple. Lead me, O LORD, in thy righteousness because of mine enemies; make thy way straight before my face. For there is NO FAITHFULNESS in their mouth; their i-n-w-a-r-d part is VERY WICKEDNESS; their throat is an open sepulchre; they flatter with their tongue. **Destroy thou them, O God; let them fall by their own counsels; cast them out in the multitude of their transgressions; for they have rebelled against thee.** *But let all those that put their trust in thee REJOICE: let them ever shout for JOY, because thou defendest them: let them also that love thy name be JOYFUL in thee. For thou, LORD, wilt bless the righteous; with favour wilt thou* *compass him as with a shield.* (Psalm 5:1-12)

The **FOOL** hath said in his heart, THERE IS NO GOD. THEY ARE CORRUPT, THEY HAVE DONE ABOMINABLE WORKS, THERE IS NONE THAT DOETH GOOD. The LORD looked down from heaven upon the children of men, to see if there were *any* that did *understand, and seek* God. THEY ARE ALL GONE ASIDE, THEY ARE ALL TOGETHER BECOME FILTHY: THERE IS NONE THAT DOETH GOOD, NO, NOT ONE. **Have all the workers of iniquity** *no* **knowledge?** who eat up my people as they eat bread, and call *not* upon the LORD. There were they in great fear: *for God is in the generation of the righteous.* Ye have shamed the counsel of the poor, because the LORD is his refuge. Oh that the salvation of Israel were come out of Zion! when the LORD bringeth back the captivity of his people, Jacob shall rejoice, and Israel shall be glad. (Psalm 14:1-7)

O Lord, rebuke me *not* in thy WRATH: neither chasten me in thy HOT displeasure. *For* thine arrows stick fast in me, and thy hand presseth me sore. There is no soundness in my flesh *because* of THINE ANGER; neither is there any rest in my bones *because* of MY SIN. *For* MINE INIQUITIES ARE GONE OVER MINE HEAD: as an heavy burden they are too heavy for me. My WOUNDS stink and are corrupt because of my **FOOLISHNESS.** I am troubled; I am bowed down greatly; I go mourning all the day long. For my loins are filled with a loathsome disease: and there is no soundness in my flesh. I am feeble and sore broken: I have roared by reason of the disquietness of my heart. *Lord, all my desire is before thee; and my groaning is not hid from thee.* My heart panteth, my strength faileth me: as for the light of mine eyes, it also is gone from me. My lovers and my friends stand aloof from my sore; and my kinsmen stand afar off. They also that seek after my life lay snares for me: and they that seek my hurt speak mischievous things, and imagine deceits all the day long. But I, as a <u>deaf man</u>, *heard not*; and I was as a <u>dumb man</u> that *openeth not his mouth*. ***Thus*** I was as a man that <u>heareth not</u>, and in whose mouth are <u>no reproofs</u>. *For in thee, O LORD, do I hope: thou wilt hear, O Lord my God.* For I said, Hear me, lest otherwise they should rejoice over me: when my foot slippeth, they magnify themselves against me. For I am ready to halt, and my sorrow is continually before me. *For* I WILL DECLARE MINE INIQUITY; I WILL BE SORRY FOR MY SIN. *But* mine enemies are lively, and they are strong: and <u>they that hate me wrongfully are multiplied</u>. **They also that render evil for good are mine adversaries;** *because* **I follow the thing that good is.** *Forsake me not, O LORD: O my God, be not far from me. Make haste to help me, O Lord my salvation.* (Psalm 38:1-22)

I said, I WILL TAKE HEED TO MY WAYS, THAT I SIN NOT WITH MY TONGUE: I WILL KEEP MY MOUTH WITH A BRIDLE, while the wicked is before me. I was dumb with silence, I held my peace, even from good; and my sorrow was stirred. My heart was HOT within me, while I was musing the fire burned: then spake I with my tongue, <u>LORD, make me to know *mine* end, and the measure of *my* days, what it is: that I may know how frail *I* am</u>. Behold, thou hast made my days as an handbreadth; and mine age is as nothing before thee: VERILY EVERY MAN AT HIS BEST STATE IS ALTOGETHER V-A-N-I-T-Y. Selah. Surely every man walketh in a VAIN shew: surely they are disquieted in VAIN: he heapeth up riches, and knoweth not who shall gather them. And now, Lord, what wait I for? *my hope is in thee.* DELIVER ME FROM ALL MY TRANSGRESSIONS: make me *not* the reproach of the **FOOLISH.** I was dumb, I opened not my mouth; because thou didst it. REMOVE THY STROKE AWAY FROM ME: I AM CONSUMED BY THE BLOW OF THINE HAND. *When* **thou with rebukes dost correct man for iniquity,** thou makest his beauty to consume away like a moth: surely every man is VANITY. Selah. Hear my prayer, O LORD, and give ear unto my cry; hold not thy peace at my tears: for I am a stranger with thee, and a sojourner, as all my fathers were. **O spare me,** that I may recover strength, before I go hence, and be no more. (Psalm 39:1-13)

Hear this, all ye people; give ear, all ye inhabitants of the world: Both low and high, rich and poor, together. *My mouth shall speak of wisdom; and the meditation of my heart shall be of understanding.* I will incline mine ear to a PARABLE: I will open my dark saying upon the harp. Wherefore should I fear in the days of evil, when the iniquity of my heels shall compass me about? **They that trust in their wealth, and boast themselves in the multitude of their riches;** *None* of them can by any means redeem his brother, nor give to God a ransom for him: (For the redemption of their soul is *precious,* and it ceaseth for ever:) That he should still live for ever, and not see corruption. *For* HE

SEETH THAT WISE MEN DIE, LIKEWISE THE **FOOL** and THE BRUTISH PERSON PERISH, and LEAVE THEIR WEALTH TO OTHERS. Their inward thought is, that their houses shall continue for ever, and their dwelling places to all generations; they call their lands after their own names. *Nevertheless* MAN BEING IN HONOUR ABIDETH NOT: **he is like the beasts that perish.** THIS THEIR WAY IS THEIR FOLLY: yet their posterity approve their sayings. Selah. Like sheep they are laid in the grave; death shall feed on them; and the upright shall have dominion over them in the morning; and their beauty shall consume in the grave from their dwelling. *But God will redeem my soul from the power of the grave: for he shall receive me.* Selah. Be not thou afraid when one is made rich, when the glory of his house is increased; **For when he dieth he shall carry NOTHING away: his glory shall not descend after him.** Though while he lived he blessed *his* soul: and men will praise thee, when thou doest well to thyself. He shall go to the generation of his fathers; T-H-E-Y  S-H-A-L-L  N-E-V-E-R  S-E-E  L-I-G-H-T. **Man that is in honour, and understandeth *not*, is like the beasts that perish.** (Psalm 49:1-20)

The **FOOL** hath said in his heart, THERE IS NO GOD. CORRUPT ARE THEY, and HAVE DONE A-B-O-M-I-N-A-B-L-E  I-N-I-Q-U-I-T-Y: **there is *none* that doeth good.** God looked down from heaven upon the children of men, to see if there were *any* that did understand, that did seek God. EVERY ONE OF THEM IS GONE BACK: THEY ARE ALTOGETHER BECOME FILTHY; THERE IS NONE THAT DOETH GOOD, NO,

NOT ONE. **Have the workers of iniquity *no* knowledge?** who eat up my people as they eat bread: THEY HAVE NOT CALLED UPON GOD. There were they in great fear, where **NO FEAR WAS:** for God hath scattered the bones of him that encampeth against thee: thou hast put them to shame, ***b-e-c-a-u-s-e*** G-O-D H-A-T-H D-E-S-P-I-S-E-D T-H-E-M. (Psalm 53:1-5)

SAVE ME, O GOD; for the waters are come in unto my soul. I sink in deep mire, where there is no standing: I am come into deep waters, where the floods overflow me. I am weary of my crying: my throat is dried: mine eyes fail while I wait for my God. They that hate me **without a cause** are more than the hairs of mine head: they that would destroy me, being mine enemies **wrongfully,** are mighty: then I restored that which I took not away. O GOD, THOU KNOWEST MY **FOOLISHNESS;** *and* MY SINS ARE NOT HID FROM THEE. (Psalm 69:1-5)

Truly God is good to Israel, even to such as are of a *clean heart*. **But** as for me, MY FEET WERE ALMOST GONE; MY STEPS HAD WELL NIGH SLIPPED. *For* I WAS ENVIOUS AT THE **FOOLISH,** WHEN I SAW THE PROSPERITY OF THE WICKED. For there are *no* bands in their death: but their strength is firm. They are *not* in trouble as other men; *neither* are they plagued like other men. Therefore PRIDE compasseth them about as a chain; VIOLENCE covereth them as a garment. Their eyes stand out with FATNESS: they have more than heart could wish. They are CORRUPT, and SPEAK WICKEDLY concerning oppression: they SPEAK LOFTILY. They set their mouth against the heavens, and their tongue walketh through the earth. Therefore his people return hither: and waters of a full cup are wrung out to them. And they say, HOW DOTH GOD KNOW? *and* IS THERE KNOWLEDGE IN THE MOST HIGH? Behold, these are the UNGODLY, who prosper in the world; they increase in riches. Verily I have cleansed my heart in VAIN, and washed my hands in innocency. **For ALL the day long have I been plagued, and chastened EVERY morning.** If I say, I will speak thus; behold, I should offend against the generation of thy children. When I thought to know this, it was too painful for me; U-N-T-I-L I WENT INTO THE SANCTUARY OF GOD; T-H-E-N UNDERSTOOD I THEIR END. **Surely thou didst set them in slippery places: thou castedst them down into destruction. How are they brought into desolation, as in a moment! they are utterly consumed with terrors. As a dream when one awaketh; so, O Lord, when thou awakest, thou shalt *despise* their image.** Thus my heart was grieved, and I was pricked in my reins. SO **FOOLISH** WAS I, and IGNORANT: I WAS AS A BEAST BEFORE THEE. *Nevertheless I am continually with thee: thou hast holden me by my right hand. Thou shalt guide me with thy counsel, and afterward receive me to glory. Whom have I in heaven but thee? and there is none upon earth that I desire beside thee. My flesh and my heart faileth: but God is the strength of my heart, and my portion for ever.* For, lo, THEY THAT ARE FAR FROM THEE SHALL P-E-R-I-S-H: THOU HAST D-E-S-T-R-O-YE-D ALL THEM THAT GO A WHORING FROM THEE. ***But*** *it is good for me to draw near to God: I* *have put my trust in the Lord* GOD, *that I may declare all thy works.* (Psalm 73:1-28)

Remember this, that **the enemy hath reproached, O** LORD, *and* that the **FOOLISH** PEOPLE HAVE BLASPHEMED THY NAME. O deliver not the soul of thy turtledove unto the multitude of the WICKED: forget not the congregation of thy poor for ever. Have respect unto the covenant: **for the dark places of the earth are full of the <u>habitations of cruelty</u>.** O let not the oppressed return ashamed: let the poor and needy praise thy name. Arise, O God, plead thine own cause: *remember* how THE **FOOLISH** MAN REPROACHETH THEE DAILY. Forget not the voice of thine enemies: the tumult of those that rise up against thee increaseth <u>continually</u>. (Psalm 74:18-23)

*Unto thee, O God, do we give thanks, unto thee do we give thanks: for that thy name is near thy wondrous works declare.* When I shall receive the congregation I will judge uprightly. The earth and all the inhabitants thereof are dissolved: I bear up the pillars of it. Selah. I said unto the **FOOLS,** <u>Deal not foolishly</u>: and to the WICKED, <u>Lift not up the horn</u>: Lift not up your horn on high: <u>speak not with a stiff neck</u>. For PROMOTION cometh neither from the east, nor from the west, nor from the south. ***But*** GOD IS THE JUDGE: **he putteth down one,** *and setteth up another.* For in the hand of the LORD there is a CUP, and the wine is red; it is full of mixture; and he poureth out of the same: *but* THE DREGS THEREOF, ALL THE WICKED OF THE EARTH SHALL WRING THEM OUT, and drink them. But I will declare for ever; I will sing praises to the God of Jacob. **All the horns of the wicked also will I cut off;** *but the horns of the righteous shall be exalted.* (Psalm 75:1-10)

*It is a good thing to give thanks unto the L*ORD, *and to sing praises unto thy name, O Most High: To shew forth thy lovingkindness in the morning, and thy faithfulness every night, Upon an instrument of ten strings, and upon the psaltery; upon the harp with a solemn sound. For thou, L*ORD, *hast made me glad through thy work: I will triumph in the works of thy hands. O L*ORD, *how great are thy works! and thy thoughts are very deep.* A BRUTISH MAN KNOWETH NOT; NEITHER DOTH A **FOOL** UNDERSTAND THIS. When the WICKED spring as the grass, and when all the WORKERS OF INIQUITY do flourish; **it is that *they* shall be destroyed <u>for</u> <u>ever</u>:** But thou, LORD, art most high for evermore. <u>For, lo, thine enemies, O L</u><u>ORD</u><u>, for, lo, thine enemies shall</u> **perish;** <u>all the workers of iniquity shall be scattered</u>. But my horn shalt thou exalt like the horn of an unicorn: I shall be anointed with fresh oil. Mine eye also shall see my desire on mine enemies, and mine ears shall hear my desire of the wicked that rise up against me. *The righteous shall flourish like the palm tree: he shall grow like a cedar in Lebanon. Those that be planted in the house of the L*ORD *shall flourish in the courts of our God. They shall still bring forth fruit in old age; they shall be fat and flourishing; To shew that the L*ORD *is upright: he is my rock, and there is no unrighteousness in him.* (Psalm 92:1-15)

<u>O Lord God, to whom VENGEANCE belongeth; O God, to whom VENGEANCE belongeth, shew thyself</u>. Lift up thyself, THOU JUDGE OF THE

111

EARTH: **render a reward to the <u>proud</u>.** LORD, how long shall the <u>wicked</u>, HOW LONG SHALL THE WICKED TRIUMPH? How long shall they utter and speak hard things? *and* ALL THE WORKERS OF INIQUITY BOAST THEMSELVES? They <u>break in pieces thy people</u>, O LORD, *and* <u>afflict thine heritage</u>. <u>They slay the widow and the stranger</u>, *and* <u>murder the fatherless</u>. *Yet* they say, **The LORD shall not see, neither shall the God of Jacob regard it.** Understand, ye BRUTISH among the people: and ye **FOOLS,** WHEN WILL YE BE WISE? He that planted the ear, <u>shall he not hear</u>? he that formed the eye, <u>shall he not see</u>? He that chastiseth the heathen, <u>shall not he correct</u>? he that teacheth man knowledge, <u>shall not he know</u>? The LORD knoweth the THOUGHTS of man, <u>that they are vanity</u>. *Blessed is the man whom thou <u>chastenest</u>, O LORD, and teachest him out of thy law;* <u>That thou mayest give him rest from the days of adversity, until the pit be digged for the wicked</u>. (Psalm 94: 1-13)

*Oh that men would praise the LORD for his goodness, and for his wonderful works to the children of men!* For he hath BROKEN the gates of brass, and CUT the bars of iron in sunder. **FOOLS** *because* of their TRANSGRESSION, and *because* of their INIQUITIES, are **af-f-l-i-c-t-e-d.** Their soul abhorreth all manner of meat; and they draw near unto the gates of death. *T-h-e-n* **they cry unto the LORD in their trouble**, *and he saveth them out of their distresses. <u>He sent his word, and healed them, and delivered them from their destructions</u>. Oh that men would praise the LORD for his goodness, and*

*for his wonderful works to the children of men!*
(Psalm 107:15-21)

The proverbs of Solomon the son of David, king of Israel; *To know WISDOM and INSTRUCTION; to perceive the words of UNDERSTANDING; To receive the instruction of WISDOM, JUSTICE, and JUDGMENT, and EQUITY;* To give <u>subtilty to the simple</u>, to <u>the young man knowledge and discretion</u>. *A WISE MAN WILL HEAR, and WILL INCREASE LEARNING; and A MAN OF <u>UNDERSTANDING</u> SHALL ATTAIN UNTO WISE COUNSELS:* To understand a proverb, and the interpretation; the words of the wise, and their dark sayings. ***The FEAR OF THE LORD is the beginning of knowledge: but** **F-O-O-L-S <u>despise</u> wisdom and instruction.** My son, hear the instruction of thy father, and forsake not the law of thy mother: For they shall be an ornament of grace unto thy head, and chains about thy neck. My son, *if* sinners entice thee, **<u>consent thou not</u>**. *If* they say, Come with us, let us lay wait for blood, let us lurk privily for the innocent without cause: Let us swallow them up alive as the grave; and whole, as those that go down into the pit: We shall find all precious substance, we shall fill our houses with spoil: Cast in thy lot among us; let us all have one purse: <u>My son, walk not thou in the way with them; refrain thy foot from their path:</u>-For their feet run to <u>evil, and make haste to shed blood</u>. Surely in vain the net is spread in the sight of any bird. **And they lay wait for their *own* blood; they lurk privily for their *own* lives.** So are the ways of EVERY one that is greedy of gain; which taketh away the life of the owners thereof. *Wisdom* crieth without; she uttereth her voice in the streets: She crieth in the chief place

113

of concourse, in the openings of the gates: in the city she uttereth her words, saying, HOW LONG, YE SIMPLE ONES, WILL YE <u>LOVE SIMPLICITY</u>? and THE SCORNERS <u>DELIGHT IN THEIR SCORNING</u>, and **FOOLS** <u>HATE KNOWLEDGE</u>? T-U-R-N Y-O-U A-T M-Y R-E-P-R-O-O-F: *behold, I will pour out my spirit unto you, I will make known my words unto you.* Because I have called, and ye REFUSED; I have stretched out my hand, and NO MAN REGARDED; *But* ye have SET AT NOUGHT ALL MY COUNSEL, and would NONE OF MY REPROOF:

# I ALSO WILL <u>LAUGH</u> AT YOUR

# CALAMITY;

# I WILL <u>MOCK</u> WHEN YOUR FEAR COMETH;

When your fear cometh as desolation, and your destruction cometh as a whirlwind; when distress and anguish cometh upon you. *T-h-e-n* <u>shall they call upon me</u>, *b-u-t* I WILL NOT ANSWER; <u>they shall seek me early</u>, *b-u-t* THEY SHALL NOT FIND ME: *F-o-r* THAT THEY HATED KNOWLEDGE, and DID NOT CHOOSE THE

FEAR OF THE LORD: THEY WOULD NONE OF MY COUNSEL: THEY DESPISED ALL MY REPROOF. *T-h-e-r-e-f-o-r-e* SHALL THEY EAT OF THE FRUIT OF THEIR OWN WAY, and BE FILLED WITH THEIR OWN DEVICES. FOR THE TURNING AWAY OF THE SIMPLE SHALL S-L-A-Y THEM, and THE PROSPERITY OF **FOOLS** SHALL D-E-S-T-R-O-Y THEM. *B-u-t whoso hearkeneth unto me shall dwell safely, and shall be quiet from fear of evil.* (Proverbs 1:1-33)

For the FROWARD is A-B-O-M-I-N-A-T-I-O-N to the LORD: *but* his secret is with the righteous. **The curse of the LORD** is in the house of the WICKED: *but* he blesseth the habitation of the *JUST.* Surely he SCORNETH THE SCORNERS: *but* he giveth *grace unto the lowly. The wise shall inherit glory:* **but** SHAME SHALL BE THE PROMOTION OF **FOOLS.** (Proverbs 3:32-35)

*My son, keep my words, and lay up my commandments with thee. Keep my commandments, and live; and my law as the apple of thine eye. Bind them upon thy fingers, write them upon the table of thine heart. Say unto wisdom, Thou art my sister; and call understanding thy kinswoman:* That they may keep thee from the STRANGE WOMAN, from the stranger which FLATTERETH with her words. For at the window of my house I looked through my casement, And beheld among the SIMPLE ONES, I discerned among the youths, **a young man void of understanding,** Passing through the street near her corner; and he went the way to her house, In the twilight, in the evening, in the black and dark night: And, behold, there met him a woman with the attire of an harlot, and

115

SUBTIL OF HEART. (She is loud and stubborn; her feet abide not in her house: Now is she without, now in the streets, and lieth in wait at every corner.) So she caught him, and kissed him, and with an impudent face said unto him, I have peace offerings with me; this day have I payed my vows. Therefore came I forth to meet thee, diligently to seek thy face, and I have found thee. I have decked my bed with coverings of tapestry, with carved works, with fine linen of Egypt. I have perfumed my bed with myrrh, aloes, and cinnamon. Come, let us take our fill of love until the morning: let us solace ourselves with loves. For the goodman is not at home, he is gone a long journey: He hath taken a bag of money with him, and will come home at the day appointed. **With her much fair speech she caused him to YIELD, with the flattering of her lips she FORCED him.** HE GOETH AFTER HER STRAIGHTWAY, AS AN OX GOETH TO THE SLAUGHTER, OR AS A **FOOL** TO THE CORRECITON OF THE STOCKS; Till a dart strike through his liver; as a bird hasteth to the snare, and knoweth not that it is for his life. Hearken unto me now therefore, O ye children, and attend to the words of my mouth. Let *not* thine heart decline to her ways, go not astray in her paths. *For* SHE HATH CAST DOWN MANY WOUNDED: *yea,* MANY STRONG MEN HAVE BEEN SLAIN BY HER. HER HOUSE IS THE WAY TO H-E-L-L, GOING DOWN TO THE CHAMBERS OF DEATH. (Proverbs 7:1-27)

Doth not wisdom cry? and understanding put forth her voice? She standeth in the top of high places, by the way in the places of the paths. She crieth at the gates, at the entry of the city, at the coming in at the doors. UNTO YOU, O <u>MEN</u>, I CALL; and MY VOICE IS TO THE SONS OF MAN. O YE <u>SIMPLE</u>, UNDERSTAND WISDOM, and YE **FOOLS,** BE YE OF AN UNDERSTANDING HEART. *Hear; for I will speak of excellent things; and the opening of my lips shall be right things. For my mouth shall speak TRUTH; and wickedness is an abomination to my lips. All the words of my mouth are in RIGHTEOUSNESS; there is **nothing** froward or perverse in them. They are all plain to him that understandeth, and right to them that find knowledge. Receive my instruction, and not silver; and knowledge rather than choice gold. For wisdom is better than rubies; and all the things that may be desired are not to be compared to it. I wisdom dwell with PRUDENCE, and find out knowledge of witty inventions.* **The fear of the L<small>ORD</small> is to <u>h-a-t-e</u> <u>evil</u>: <u>pride</u>, and <u>arrogancy</u>, and the <u>evil way</u>, and the <u>froward mouth</u>, do I *h-a-t-e*.** *Counsel is mine, and sound wisdom: I am understanding; I have strength.* (Proverbs 8:10-14)

*Wisdom hath builded her house,* she hath hewn out her SEVEN PILLARS: She hath <u>killed her beasts</u>; she hath <u>mingled her wine</u>; she hath also <u>furnished her table</u>. She hath <u>sent forth her maidens</u>: she crieth upon the highest places of the city, WHOSO IS SIMPLE, LET HIM TURN IN HITHER: as for him that wanteth understanding, she saith to him, Come, eat of my bread, and drink of the wine which I have mingled. FORSAKE THE **FOOLISH,** *and* LIVE, *and* GO IN THE WAY OF UNDERSTANDING. **He that reproveth a <u>scorner</u> getteth to himself shame: and he that rebuketh a <u>wicked</u> man getteth himself a blot. Reprove *not* a scorner, lest he *hate* thee:** *rebuke a <u>wise man</u>, and* *he will love thee. Give instruction to a wise man, and he will be yet wiser: teach a just man, and he will increase in learning.* **The fear of the LORD is the beginning of wisdom: and the knowledge of the holy is understanding.** For by me thy days shall be multiplied, and the years of thy life shall be increased. If thou be wise, thou shalt be wise for thyself: *but* if thou scornest, thou alone shalt bear it. A **FOOLISH** WOMAN is clamorous: she is simple, and knoweth nothing. For she sitteth at the door of her house, on a seat in the high places of the city, To call passengers who go right on their ways: Whoso is simple, let him turn in hither: and as for him that wanteth understanding, she saith to him, Stolen waters are sweet, and bread eaten in secret is pleasant. But he knoweth not that the dead are there; and that HER GUESTS ARE IN THE DEPTHS OF HELL. (Proverbs 9:1-18)

**The proverbs of Solomon.** *A wise son maketh a glad father:* **but** a foolish son is the heaviness of his mother. Treasures of wickedness profit nothing: **but** *righteousness delivereth from death. The LORD will not suffer the soul of the righteous to famish:* **but** he casteth away the substance of the wicked. He becometh poor that dealeth with a slack hand: **but** *the hand of the diligent maketh rich. He that gathereth in summer is a wise son:* **but** he that sleepeth in harvest is a son that causeth shame. *Blessings are upon the head of the just:* **but** violence covereth the mouth of the wicked. *The memory of the just is blessed:* **but** the name of the wicked shall rot. *The wise in heart will receive commandments:* **but** a prating fool shall fall. *He that walketh uprightly walketh surely:* **but** he that perverteth his ways shall be known. He that winketh with the eye causeth sorrow: *but* a prating fool shall fall. *The mouth of a righteous man is a well of life:* *but* violence covereth the mouth of the wicked. Hatred stirreth up strifes: *but love covereth all sins. In the lips of him that hath understanding wisdom is found:* *but* a rod is for the back of him that is void of understanding. *Wise men lay up knowledge:* *but* the mouth of the foolish is near destruction. The rich man's wealth is his strong city: the destruction of the poor is their poverty. *The labour of the righteous tendeth to life:* the fruit of the wicked to sin. *He is in the way of life that keepeth instruction:* *but* he that refuseth reproof erreth. He that hideth hatred with lying lips, *and* he that uttereth a slander, is a **FOOL.** In the multitude of words there wanteth not sin: *but* he that refraineth his lips is wise. *The tongue of the just is as choice silver:* the heart of the wicked is little worth. *The lips of the righteous feed many:* *but* fools die for want of wisdom. *The blessing of the LORD, it maketh rich, and he addeth no sorrow with it.* It is as sport to a **FOOL** to do mischief: *but a man of understanding hath wisdom.* The fear of the wicked, it shall come upon him: *but the desire of the righteous shall be granted.* As the whirlwind passeth, so is the wicked no more: *but the righteous is an everlasting foundation.* As vinegar to the teeth, and as smoke to the eyes, so is the sluggard to them that send him. ***The fear of the LORD prolongeth days:*** *but* the years of the wicked shall be shortened. *The hope of the righteous shall be gladness:* *but* the expectation of the wicked shall perish. *The way of the LORD is strength to the upright:* *but* destruction shall be to the workers of iniquity. *The righteous shall never be removed:* *but* the wicked shall not inhabit the earth. *The mouth of* *the just bringeth forth wisdom:* **but** the froward tongue shall be cut out. *The lips of the righteous know what is acceptable:* **but** the mouth of the wicked speaketh frowardness. (Proverbs 10:1-32)

*He that diligently seeketh good procureth favour:* **but** he that seeketh mischief, it shall come unto him. He that trusteth in his riches shall fall; **but** *the righteous shall flourish as a branch.* He that troubleth his own house shall inherit the wind: **and** the **FOOL** shall be servant to the wise of heart. *The fruit of the righteous is a tree of life;* **and** *he that winneth souls is wise.* Behold, **the righteous shall be RECOMPENSED in the earth:** **MUCH MORE the wicked and the sinner.** (Proverbs 11:27-31)

The way of a **FOOL** is right in his own eyes: **but** *he that hearkeneth unto counsel is wise.* A **FOOL'S** wrath is presently known: **but** *a prudent man covereth shame.* He that speaketh truth sheweth forth righteousness: **but** a false witness deceit. There is that speaketh like the piercings of a sword: **but** *the tongue of the wise is health.* The lip of truth shall be established for ever: **but** *a lying tongue is but for a moment.* Deceit is in the heart of them that imagine evil: **but** *to the counsellors of peace is joy. There shall no evil happen to the just:* **but** the wicked shall be filled with mischief. Lying lips are ABOMINATION to the LORD: **but** *they that deal truly are his delight. A prudent man concealeth knowledge:* **but** the heart of fools proclaimeth foolishness. *The hand of the diligent shall bear rule:* **but** the slothful shall be under tribute. Heaviness in the heart of man maketh it stoop: **but** *a good word maketh it glad. The righteous is more excellent than his neighbour:* **but** the way of the wicked seduceth them. The slothful man roasteth not that which he took in hunting: *but the substance of a diligent man is precious. In the way of righteousness is life: and in the pathway thereof there is no death.* (Proverbs 12:15-28)

Whoso despiseth the word shall be destroyed: *but he that feareth the commandment shall be rewarded. The law of the wise is a fountain of life, to depart from the snares of death.* Good understanding giveth favour: *but* the way of transgressors is hard. *Every prudent man dealeth with knowledge: but* a **FOOL** layeth open his folly. A wicked messenger falleth into mischief: *but a faithful ambassador is health.* Poverty and shame shall be to him that refuseth instruction: *but he that regardeth reproof shall be honoured. The desire accomplished is sweet to the soul: but* it is abomination to **FOOLS** to depart from evil. *He that walketh with wise men shall be wise: but* a companion of **FOOLS** shall be destroyed. Evil pursueth sinners: *but to the righteous good shall be repayed. A good man leaveth an inheritance to his children's children: and* the wealth of the sinner is laid up for the just. *Much food is in the tillage of the poor: but* there is that is destroyed for want of judgment. He that spareth his rod hateth his son: *but he that loveth him chasteneth him betimes. The righteous eateth to the satisfying of his soul: but* the belly of the wicked shall want. (Proverbs 13:13-25)

*Every wise woman buildeth her house: but* the **FOOLISH** plucketh it down with her hands. *He that walketh in his uprightness* ***feareth the LORD: but*** he that is perverse in his ways despiseth him. In the mouth of the **FOOLISH** is a rod of pride: *but* *the lips of the wise shall preserve them.* Where no oxen are, the crib is clean*: but much increase is by the strength of the ox. A faithful witness will not lie: but* a false witness will utter lies. A scorner seeketh wisdom, and findeth it not: *but knowledge is easy unto him that understandeth.* Go from the presence of a foolish man, when thou perceivest *not* in him the lips of knowledge. *The wisdom of the prudent is to understand his way: but* the folly of **FOOLS** is deceit. **FOOLS** make a mock at sin: *but among the righteous there is favour.* The heart knoweth his own bitterness; and a stranger doth *not* intermeddle with his joy. The house of the wicked shall be overthrown: *but the tabernacle of the upright shall flourish.* There is a way which seemeth right unto a man, **but** the end thereof are the ways of death. Even in laughter the heart is sorrowful; *and* the end of that mirth is heaviness. The backslider in heart shall be filled with his own ways: *and a good man shall be satisfied from himself.* The simple believeth every word: *but the prudent man looketh well to his going. A wise man feareth, and departeth from evil: but* the fool rageth, and is confident. He that is soon angry dealeth foolishly: *and* a man of wicked devices is hated. The simple inherit folly: *but the prudent are crowned with knowledge. The evil bow before the good; and the wicked at the gates of the righteous.* The poor is hated even of his own neighbour: *but* the rich hath many friends. He that despiseth his neighbour sinneth: *but he that hath mercy on the poor, happy is he.* Do they not err that devise evil? *but mercy and truth shall be to them that devise good. In all labour there is profit: but* the talk of the lips tendeth only to penury. *The crown of the wise is their riches: but* the foolishness of **FOOLS** is folly. *A true witness delivereth souls:*

*but* <u>a deceitful witness speaketh lies.</u> *In **the fear of the** L*ORD* is strong confidence: **and** his children shall have a place of refuge. **The fear of the** L*ORD* is a fountain of life, to depart from the snares of death. In the multitude of people is the king's honour: **but** <u>in the want of people is the destruction of the prince.</u> He that is slow to wrath is of great understanding: **but** <u>he that is hasty of spirit exalteth folly.</u> A sound heart is the life of the flesh: **but** <u>envy the rottenness of the bones.</u> He that oppresseth the poor reproacheth his Maker: **but** he that honoureth him hath mercy on the poor. The wicked is driven away in his wickedness: **but** the righteous hath hope in his death. Wisdom resteth in the heart of him that hath understanding: **but** <u>that which is in the midst of</u> **FOOLS** <u>is made known.</u> Righteousness exalteth a nation: **but** <u>sin is a reproach to any people.</u> The king's favour is toward a wise servant: **but** <u>his wrath is against him that causeth shame.</u>  (Proverbs 14:1-35)*

*A soft answer turneth away wrath: **but** <u>grievous words stir up anger.</u> The tongue of the wise useth knowledge aright: **but** <u>the mouth of fools poureth out foolishness.</u>* THE EYES OF THE LORD ARE IN E-V-E-R-Y PLACE, BEHOLDING THE EVIL and THE GOOD. *A wholesome tongue is a tree of life: **but** <u>perverseness therein is a breach in the spirit.</u> A* **FOOL** <u>despiseth his father's instruction:</u> *but* he that regardeth reproof is prudent. In the house of the righteous is much treasure: **but** <u>in the revenues of the wicked is trouble.</u> The lips of the wise disperse knowledge: **but** <u>the heart of the foolish doeth not so.</u>* **The sacrifice of the wicked is an a-b-o-m-i-n-a-t-i-o-n to the** L*ORD***: *but* the prayer of the upright is his delight.* **The way of the**

**wicked is an a-b-o-m-i-n-a-t-i-o-n unto the LORD:** *but he loveth him that followeth after righteousness.* Correction is grievous unto him that forsaketh the way: *and* he that hateth reproof shall die. HELL and DESTRUCTION ARE BEFORE THE LORD: HOW MUCH MORE THEN THE HEARTS OF THE CHILDREN OF MEN? A scorner loveth not one that reproveth him: *neither will he go unto the wise.* *A merry heart maketh a cheerful countenance: but* by sorrow of the heart the spirit is broken. *The heart of him that hath understanding seeketh knowledge: but* the mouth of **FOOLS** feedeth on **FOOLISHNESS.** All the days of the afflicted are evil: *but he that is of a merry heart hath a continual feast. Better is little with the fear of the LORD than* great treasure and trouble therewith. *Better is a dinner of herbs where love is, than* a stalled ox and hatred therewith. A wrathful man stirreth up strife: *but he that is slow to anger appeaseth strife.* The way of the slothful man is as an hedge of thorns: *but the way of the righteous is made plain.* *A wise son maketh a glad father: but* a **FOOLISH** man despiseth his mother. (Proverbs 15:1-20)

*Understanding is a wellspring of life unto him that hath it: but* the instruction of **FOOLS** is folly. (Proverbs 16:22)

*Better is a dry morsel, and quietness therewith, than* an house full of sacrifices with strife. *A wise servant shall have rule over a son that causeth shame, and shall have part of the inheritance among the brethren.* The fining pot is for silver, and the furnace for gold: *but* THE LORD TRIETH THE HEARTS. A wicked doer giveth heed to false lips;

*and* a liar giveth ear to a naughty tongue. Whoso mocketh the poor reproacheth his Maker: *and* he that is glad at calamities shall not be unpunished. *Children's children are the crown of old men; **and** the glory of children are their fathers.* Excellent speech becometh not a **FOOL**: much less do lying lips a prince. *A gift is as a precious stone in the eyes of him that hath it: whithersoever it turneth, it prospereth. He that covereth a transgression seeketh love; **but*** he that repeateth a matter separateth very friends. *A reproof entereth more into a wise man **than** an hundred stripes into a **FOOL**.* An evil man seeketh only rebellion: *therefore* a cruel messenger shall be sent against him. Let a bear robbed of her whelps meet a man, rather than a **FOOL** in his folly. **Whoso rewardeth evil for good, evil shall not depart from his house.** The beginning of strife is as when one letteth out water: *therefore* leave off contention, before it be meddled with. **He that justifieth the wicked, *and* he that condemneth the just, even they both are a-b-o-m-i-n-a-t-i-o-n to tho LORD.** Wherefore is there a price in the hand of a **FOOL** to get wisdom, seeing he hath no heart to it? *A friend loveth at all times, **and** a brother is born for adversity.* A man void of understanding striketh hands, *and* becometh surety in the presence of his friend. He loveth TRANSGRESSION that loveth strife: *and* he that EXALTETH HIS GATE seeketh destruction. He that hath a FROWARD heart findeth no good: *and* he that hath a PERVERSE TONGUE falleth into mischief. He that begetteth a **FOOL** doeth it to his sorrow: *and* the father of a **FOOL** hath no joy. *A merry heart doeth good like a medicine: **but*** a broken spirit drieth the bones. A wicked man taketh a gift out of the bosom to pervert the ways of judgment. *Wisdom is before him that hath understanding; **but** the eyes of a **FOOL** are in the ends of the earth. A **FOOLISH** son is a grief to his father, **and** bitterness to her that bare him. Also to punish the just is not good, **nor** to strike princes for equity. He that hath knowledge spareth his words: **and** a man of understanding is of an excellent spirit. Even a **FOOL,** when he holdeth his peace, is counted wise: **and** he that shutteth his lips is esteemed a man of understanding.*   (Proverbs 17:1-28)

Through desire a man, having separated himself, seeketh and intermeddleth with all wisdom. A **FOOL** hath no delight in understanding, **but** that his heart may discover itself. When the wicked cometh, **then** cometh also contempt, **and** with ignominy reproach. *The words of a (wise) man's mouth are as deep waters, **and** the wellspring of wisdom as a flowing brook.* It is not good to accept the person of the wicked, to overthrow the righteous in judgment. A **FOOL'S** lips enter into contention, **and** his mouth calleth for strokes. A **FOOL'S** mouth is his destruction, **and** his lips are the snare of his soul. The words of a talebearer are as wounds, **and** they go down into the innermost parts of the belly. He also that is slothful in his work is brother to him that is a great waster.  (Proverbs 18:1-9)

*Better is the poor that walketh in his integrity, **than** he that is perverse in his lips, **and** is a **FOOL.** Also, that the soul be without knowledge, it is not good; **and** he that hasteth with his feet sinneth.* The **FOOLISHNESS** of man perverteth his way: **and** his heart fretteth against the LORD. Wealth maketh many friends; **but** the poor is separated from his neighbour. <u>A false witness shall not be unpunished,</u> **and** <u>he that speaketh lies shall not escape.</u> Many will intreat the favour of the prince: **and** every man is a friend to him that giveth gifts. All the brethren of the poor do hate him: how much more do his friends go far from him? he pursueth them with words, **yet** they are wanting to him. *He that getteth wisdom loveth his own soul: he that keepeth understanding shall find good.* <u>A false witness shall not be unpunished,</u> **and** <u>he that speaketh lies shall perish.</u> <u>Delight is not seemly for a</u> **FOOL;** <u>much less for a servant to have rule over princes.</u> *The discretion of a man deferreth his anger;* **and** *it is his glory to pass over a transgression.* <u>The king's wrath is as the roaring of a lion;</u> **but** *his favour is as dew upon the grass.* <u>A</u> **FOOLISH** <u>son is the calamity of his father:</u> **and** <u>the contentions of a wife are a continual dropping.</u> *House and riches are the inheritance of fathers:* **and** *a prudent wife is from the* LORD. <u>Slothfulness casteth into a deep sleep;</u> **and** <u>an idle soul shall suffer hunger.</u> *He that keepeth the commandment keepeth his own soul;* **but** <u>he that despiseth his ways shall die.</u> *He that hath pity upon the poor lendeth unto the* LORD; **and** *that which he hath given will he pay him again.* CHASTEN THY SON WHILE THERE IS HOPE, **and** LET NOT THY SOUL SPARE FOR HIS CRYING. <u>A man of great wrath shall suffer punishment:</u> *for* <u>if thou deliver him, yet thou must do it again.</u> *Hear counsel, and receive instruction,* **that** *thou mayest be wise in thy latter end.* <u>There are many devices in a man's heart;</u> **nevertheless** THE COUNSEL OF THE LORD, THAT SHALL STAND. *The desire of a man is his kindness:* **and** *a poor man is better than a liar.* **The fear of the LORD** *tendeth to life:* **and** *he that hath it shall abide satisfied; he shall not* *be visited with evil.* A slothful man hideth his hand in his bosom, *and* will not so much as bring it to his mouth again. Smite a scorner, *and* the simple will beware: *and reprove one that hath understanding, and he will understand knowledge.* He that wasteth his father, *and* chaseth away his mother, is a son that causeth shame, and bringeth reproach. CEASE, my son, to hear the instruction that causeth to err from the words of knowledge. An ungodly witness scorneth judgment: *and* the mouth of the wicked devoureth iniquity. Judgments are prepared for scorners, *and* stripes for the back of **FOOLS**. (Proverbs 19:1-29)

Wine is a mocker, strong drink is raging: *and* whosoever is deceived thereby is not wise. The fear of a king is as the roaring of a lion: whoso provoketh him to anger sinneth against his own soul. *It is an honour for a man to cease from strife:* *but* every **FOOL** will be meddling. The sluggard will not plow by reason of the cold; *therefore* shall he beg in harvest, and have nothing.   (Proverbs 20:1-4)

*It is joy to the just to do judgment:* **but** destruction shall be to the workers of iniquity. The man that wandereth out of the way of understanding shall remain in the congregation of the dead. He that loveth pleasure shall be a poor man: he that loveth wine and oil shall *not* be rich. *The wicked shall be a ransom for the righteous,* ***and*** *the transgressor for the upright.* It is better to dwell in the wilderness, ***than*** with a contentious and an angry woman. *There is treasure to be desired and oil in the dwelling of the wise;* ***but*** a **FOOLISH** man spendeth it up. (Proverbs 21:15-20)

**FOOLISHNESS** is bound in the heart of a child; *but* THE ROD OF CORRECTION SHALL DRIVE IT FAR FROM HIM. (Proverbs 22:15)

Speak not in the ears of a **FOOL:** *for* HE WILL DESPISE THE WISDOM OF THY WORDS. Proverbs 23:9)

Be not thou envious against evil men, *neither* desire to be with them. *For* their heart studieth destruction, *and* their lips talk of mischief. *Through wisdom is an house builded; and by understanding it is established: And by knowledge shall the chambers be filled with all precious and pleasant riches. A wise man is strong; yea, a man of knowledge increaseth strength. For by wise counsel thou shalt make thy war: and in multitude of counsellors there is safety.* Wisdom is too high for a **FOOL:** he openeth not his mouth in the gate. He that deviseth to do evil shall be called a mischievous person. The thought of **FOOLISHNESS** is sin: *and* the scorner is an **abomination** to men. (Proverbs 24:1-9)

As snow in summer, and as rain in harvest, so honour is *not* seemly for a **FOOL.** *As the bird by wandering, as the swallow by flying, so the curse causeless shall not come.* A whip for the horse, a bridle for the ass, and a rod for the **FOOL'S** back. Answer not a **FOOL** according to his folly, lest thou also be like unto him. Answer a **FOOL** according to his folly, lest he be wise in his own conceit. He that sendeth a message by the hand of a **FOOL** cutteth off the feet, and drinketh damage. The legs of the lame are not equal: so is a parable in the mouth of **FOOLS.** As he that bindeth a stone in a sling, so is he that giveth honour to a

**FOOL.** As a thorn goeth up into the hand of a drunkard, so is a parable in the mouths of **FOOLS.** The great God that formed all things both rewardeth the **FOOL,** and rewardeth transgressors. As a dog returneth to his vomit, so a **FOOL** returneth to his folly. Seest thou a man wise in his own conceit? there is more hope of a **FOOL** than of him. (Proverbs 26:1-12)

A stone is heavy, and the sand weighty; *but* a **FOOL'S** wrath is heavier than them both. Wrath is cruel, and anger is outrageous; *but* who is able to stand before envy? Open rebuke is better than secret love. *Faithful are the wounds of a friend; but* the kisses of an enemy are deceitful. The full soul loatheth an honeycomb; *but to the hungry soul every bitter thing is sweet.* As a bird that wandereth from her nest, so is a man that wandereth from his place. Ointment and perfume rejoice the heart: *so doth the sweetness of a man's friend by hearty counsel.* Thine own friend, and thy father's friend, *forsake not;* neither go into thy brother's house in the day of thy calamity: *for better is a neighbour that is near* than a brother far off. My son, be wise, and make my heart glad, that I may answer him that reproacheth me. *A prudent man foreseeth the evil, and hideth himself; b-u-t* **the simple pass on, and are punished.** Take his garment that is surety for a stranger, and take a pledge of him for a strange woman. He that blesseth his friend with a loud voice, rising early in the morning, it shall be counted a curse to him. A continual dropping in a very rainy day and a contentious woman are alike. Whosoever hideth her hideth the wind, and the ointment of his right hand, which bewrayeth itself. *Iron sharpeneth iron; so a man sharpeneth* *the countenance of his friend.* Whoso keepeth the fig tree shall eat the fruit thereof: *so he that waiteth on his master shall be honoured.* As in water face answereth to face, *so the heart of man to man.* HELL AND DESTRUCTION ARE NEVER FULL; so the eyes of man are never satisfied. As the fining pot for silver, and the furnace for gold; so is a man to his praise. **Though thou shouldest bray a FOOL in a mortar among wheat with a pestle, *yet* will not his FOOLISHNESS depart from him.** (Proverbs 27: 3-22)

He that trusteth in his own heart is a **FOOL:** *but whoso walketh wisely, he shall be delivered. He that giveth unto the poor shall not lack:* **but** he that hideth his eyes shall have many a curse. When the wicked rise, men hide themselves: *but* when they perish, *the righteous increase.* (Proverbs 28:26-28)

If a wise man contendeth with a **FOOLISH** man, whether he rage or laugh, there is no rest. The bloodthirsty **hate** the upright: *but the just seek his soul.* A **FOOL** uttereth all his mind: *but a wise man keepeth it in till afterwards.* If a ruler hearken to lies, all his servants are wicked. The poor and the deceitful man meet together: the LORD lighteneth both their eyes. *The king that faithfully judgeth the poor, his throne shall be established for ever. The rod and reproof give wisdom:* **but** a child left to himself bringeth his mother to shame. When the wicked are multiplied, transgression increaseth: **but** *the righteous shall see their fall.* Correct thy son, ***and*** *he shall give thee rest;* **yea,** *he shall give delight unto thy soul.* Where there is no vision, the people perish: **but** *he that keepeth the law, happy is he.* A servant will not be corrected by words: for though he understand he will not answer. <u>Seest thou a man that is HASTY in his words</u>? **there is more hope of a FOOL than of him.** (Proverbs 29:9-20)

For THREE things the earth is disquieted, and for FOUR which it cannot bear: <u>For a servant when he reigneth</u>; and <u>a **FOOL** when he is filled with meat</u>; For <u>an odious woman when she is married</u>; and <u>an handmaid that is heir to her mistress</u>. There be FOUR things which are little upon the earth, ***but they are exceeding wise:*** The ANTS are a people not strong, *yet* they prepare their meat in the summer; The CONIES are but a feeble folk, *yet* make they their houses in the rocks; The LOCUSTS have no king, *yet* go they forth all of them by bands; The SPIDER taketh hold with her hands, *and* is in kings' palaces. There be THREE things which go well, yea, FOUR are *comely* in going: A LION which is strongest among beasts, *and* turneth not away for any; A GREYHOUND; an HE GOAT also; and a KING, against whom there is no rising up. **If thou hast done FOOLISHLY in lifting up thyself,** *or* **if thou hast thought evil, <u>lay thine hand upon thy mouth.</u>** Surely <u>the churning of milk bringeth forth butter</u>, and <u>the wringing of the nose bringeth forth blood: so the forcing of wrath bringeth forth strife</u>. (Proverbs 30:21-33)

Ye have heard that it was said of them of old time, Thou shalt not KILL; and whosoever shall kill shall be in danger of the judgment: ***But*** I say unto you, That WHOSOEVER IS <u>ANGRY</u> WITH HIS BROTHER WITHOUT A CAUSE SHALL BE IN DANGER OF THE JUDGMENT: *and* whosoever shall say to his brother, <u>Raca</u>, SHALL BE IN DANGER OF THE COUNCIL: *but* whosoever shall say, **THOU FOOL, SHALL BE IN DANGER OF HELL FIRE.** Therefore if thou bring thy gift to the altar, and there rememberest that thy brother hath ought against thee; Leave there thy gift before the altar, and go thy way; *first be reconciled to thy brother, and then come and offer thy gift.* (Matthew 5:21-24)

**Not every one that saith unto me, Lord, Lord, shall enter into the kingdom of heaven;** *but* **he that DOETH the will of my Father which is in heaven.** *Many* will say to me in that day, Lord, Lord, have we not prophesied in thy name? and in thy name have cast out devils? and in thy name done many wonderful works? **And then will I profess unto them, I NEVER KNEW YOU: depart from me, ye that work iniquity.** *Therefore* whosoever heareth these sayings of mine, and DOETH them, I will liken him unto a WISE MAN, which built his house upon a ROCK: And the rain descended, and the floods came, and the winds blew, and BEAT upon that house; and I-T  F-E-L-L N-O-T: *for* it was founded upon a ROCK. And every one that heareth these sayings of mine, and doeth them *not,* shall be likened unto a **FOOLISH** MAN, which built his house upon the SAND: And the rain descended, and the floods came, and the winds blew, and BEAT upon that house; and I-T F-E-L-L: and *great* was the fall of it. And it came to pass, when Jesus had ended these sayings, the people were astonished at his doctrine: For he taught them as one having authority, and not as the scribes. (Matthew 7:21-29)

Ye **FOOLS** and BLIND: for whether is greater, the gold, or the temple that sanctifieth the gold? And,

Whosoever shall swear by the altar, it is nothing; but whosoever sweareth by the gift that is upon it, he is guilty. Ye **FOOLS** and BLIND: for whether is greater, the gift, or the altar that sanctifieth the gift? (Matthew 23:17-19)

Then shall the kingdom of heaven be likened unto TEN VIRGINS, <u>which took their lamps, and went forth to meet the bridegroom.</u> And FIVE of them were WISE, and FIVE were **FOOLISH.** They that were **FOOLISH** took their lamps, and **took *no* oil with them:** *But* the WISE *took oil in their vessels with their lamps.* While the bridegroom tarried, <u>they all slumbered and slept.</u> And at MIDNIGHT there was a cry made, *Behold, the bridegroom cometh; go ye out to meet him.* Then ALL those virgins arose, and trimmed their lamps. And the **FOOLISH** said unto the WISE, <u>Give us of your oil; for our lamps are gone out.</u> But the wise answered, saying, **Not so; lest there be not enough for us and you: *but* go ye rather to them that sell, and BUY FOR YOURSELVES. And while they went to buy, the bridegroom came; and they that were ready went in with him to the marriage: and THE DOOR WAS SHUT. Afterward came also the other virgins, saying, Lord, Lord, open to us. But he answered and said, Verily I say unto you, I KNOW YOU NOT.** *Watch therefore,* **for ye know neither the day nor the hour wherein the Son of man cometh.** (Matthew 25:1-13)

And he said, That which cometh OUT of the man, that **defileth the man.** For from *within*, out of the HEART of men, proceed <u>EVIL THOUGHTS, ADULTERIES, FORNICATIONS, MURDERS, THEFTS, COVETOUSNESS, WICKEDNESS,</u>

DECEIT, LASCIVIOUSNESS, an EVIL EYE, BLASPHEMY, PRIDE, **FOOLISHNESS:** All these evil things come from WITHIN, and **defile the man.** (Mark 7:20-23)

And as he spake, a certain Pharisee besought him to dine with him: and he went in, and sat down to meat. And when the Pharisee saw it, he marvelled that he had not first washed before dinner. And the Lord said unto him, Now do ye Pharisees make clean the OUTSIDE of the cup and the platter; *but* your INWARD PART IS FULL OF RAVENING and WICKEDNESS. Ye **FOOLS,** did not he that made that which is WITHOUT make that which is WITHIN also? But rather give alms of such things as ye have; and, behold, all things are clean unto you. *But* WOE unto you, Pharisees! for ye tithe mint and rue and all manner of herbs, and **pass over judgment and the love of God:** THESE OUGHT YE TO HAVE DONE, *and* NOT TO LEAVE THE OTHER UNDONE. (Luke 11:37-42)

And he spake a parable unto them, saying, The ground of a certain rich man brought forth plentifully: And he thought within himself, saying, What shall I do, because I have no room where to bestow my fruits? And he said, This will I do: I will pull down my barns, and build greater; and there will I bestow all my fruits and my goods. And I will say to my soul, Soul, thou hast much goods laid up for many years; take thine ease, eat, drink, and be merry. *But* **God said unto him, Thou FOOL, THIS NIGHT THY SOUL SHALL BE REQUIRED OF THEE: then whose shall those things be, which thou hast provided? SO IS HE THAT LAYETH UP TREASURE FOR**

135

**HIMSELF, and IS N-O-T RICH TOWARD GOD.** (Luke 12:16-21)

And the one of them, whose name was Cleopas, answering said unto him, <u>Art thou only a stranger in Jerusalem, and hast not known the things which are come to pass there in these days</u>? And he said unto them, <u>What things</u>? And they said unto him, CONCERNING JESUS OF NAZARETH, which was a prophet mighty in deed and word before God and all the people: And how the chief priests and our rulers delivered him to be condemned to death, and have crucified him. *But* we trusted that it had been he which should have redeemed Israel: and beside all this, to day is the third day since these things were done. Yea, and certain women also of our company made us astonished, which were early at the sepulchre; And when they found not his body, they came, saying, that they had also seen a vision of angels, which said that he was alive. And certain of them which were with us went to the sepulchre, and found it even so as the women had said: but him they saw not. Then he said unto them, **O F-O-O-L-S,** *and* **slow of heart** **to believe all that the prophets have spoken:** <u>Ought not Christ to have suffered these things, and to enter into his glory</u>? And beginning at Moses and all the prophets, he expounded unto them in all the scriptures the things concerning himself. (Luke 24:18-27)

**For the WRATH OF GOD is revealed from heaven against** *all* **ungodliness and unrighteousness of men, who hold the truth in unrighteousness;** *Because* that which may be known of God is manifest in them; for God hath shewed it unto them. For the *invisible things* of him from the creation of the world <u>are clearly seen,</u>

being understood by the things that are made, even his eternal power and Godhead; S-O  T-H-A-T T-H-E-Y A-R-E W-I-T-H-O-U-T E-X-C-U-S-E: Because that, when they knew God, they glorified him not as God, *neither* were <u>thankful</u>; *but* BECAME VAIN IN THEIR IMAGINATIONS, and THEIR **<u>FOOLISH</u>** HEART WAS DARKENED. Professing themselves to be wise, THEY BECAME **F-O-O-L-S,** And changed the glory of the uncorruptible God into an image made like to corruptible man, and to birds, and fourfooted beasts, and creeping things.   Wherefore **GOD ALSO GAVE THEM UP** TO UNCLEANNESS THROUGH THE LUSTS OF THEIR OWN HEARTS, TO DISHONOUR THEIR OWN BODIES BETWEEN THEMSELVES:   **Who changed the truth of God into a <u>l-i-e</u>,** and worshipped and served the creature more than the Creator, who is blessed for ever. Amen. FOR THIS CAUSE GOD GAVE THEM UP UNTO **V-I-L-E** AFFECTIONS: FOR EVEN THEIR WOMEN DID CHANGE THE NATURAL USE INTO THAT WHICH IS A-G-A-I-N-S-T NATURE: *and* LIKEWISE ALSO THE MEN, LEAVING THE NATURAL USE OF THE WOMAN, BURNED IN THEIR LUST ONE TOWARD ANOTHER; MEN WITH MEN WORKING THAT WHICH IS UNSEEMLY, and RECEIVIING IN THEMSELVES THAT R-E-C-O-M-P-E-N-C-E OF THEIR ERROR WHICH WAS MEET. **And even as they did not like to retain God in their knowledge, <u>God</u> <u>gave</u> <u>them</u> <u>over</u> <u>to</u> <u>a</u> <u>r-e-p-r-o-b-a-t-e</u>  <u>m-i-n-d</u>, to do those things which are not convenient;** BEING FILLED WITH <u>A-L-L</u> <u>UNRIGHTEOUSNESS</u>, <u>FORNICATION</u>, <u>WICKEDNESS</u>, <u>COVETOUSNESS</u>,

MALICIOUSNESS, FULL OF ENVY, MURDER, DEBATE, DECEIT, MALIGNITY; WHISPERERS, BACKBITERS, HATERS OF GOD, DESPITEFUL, PROUD, BOASTERS, INVENTORS OF EVIL THINGS, DISOBEDIENT TO PARENTS, WITHOUT UNDERSTANDING, COVENANTBREAKERS, WITHOUT NATURAL AFFECTION, IMPLACABLE, UNMERCIFUL: WHO KNOWING THE JUDGMENT OF GOD, THAT THEY WHICH COMMIT SUCH THINGS ARE WORTHY OF D-E-A-T-H, NOT ONLY DO THE SAME, *but* HAVE P-L-E-A-S-U-R-E IN THEM THAT DO THEM. (Romans 1:18-32)

EVERY MAN'S WORK SHALL BE MADE MANIFEST: for the day shall declare it, *because* IT SHALL BE REVEALED BY FIRE; and THE FIRE SHALL T-R-Y EVERY MAN'S WORK OF WHAT SORT IT IS. *If any man's work abide which he hath built thereupon,* **he shall receive a reward.** **If any man's work shall be burned, he shall suffer loss:** *but* he himself shall be saved; *yet so as by fire.* KNOW YE NOT THAT YE ARE THE TEMPLE OF GOD, and THAT THE SPIRIT OF GOD DWELLETH IN YOU? *If* **any man defile the temple of God, him shall God destroy;** *for the temple of God is holy, which temple ye are.* LET NO MAN DECEIVE HIMSELF. If any man among you seemeth to be wise in this world, LET HIM BECOME A **FOOL,** THAT HE MAY BE WISE. **For the wisdom of this world is FOOLISHNESS with God.** For it is written, **He taketh the wise in their own craftiness.** And again, **The Lord knoweth the thoughts of the wise, that they are** *vain.* (1 Corinthians 3:13-20)

AWAKE TO RIGHTEOUSNESS, and SIN NOT; for some have not the knowledge of God: I speak this to your *shame*. But some man will say, How are the dead raised up? and with what body do they come? THOU **FOOL,** that which thou sowest is not QUICKENED, except it DIE: And that which thou sowest, thou sowest not that body that shall be, but bare grain, it may chance of wheat, or of some other grain: *But God giveth it a body as it hath pleased him, and to every seed his own body.* All flesh is **not** the same flesh: but there is one kind of flesh of men, another flesh of beasts, another of fishes, and another of birds. There are also celestial bodies, and bodies terrestrial: but the glory of the celestial is one, and the glory of the terrestrial is another. There is one glory of the sun, and another glory of the moon, and another glory of the stars: for one star differeth from another star in glory. SO ALSO IS THE RESURRECTION OF THE DEAD. It is sown in CORRUPTION; it is raised in INCORRUPTION: It is sown in DISHONOUR; it is raised in GLORY: it is sown in WEAKNESS; it is raised in POWER: It is sown a NATURAL body; it is raised a SPIRITUAL body. There is a *natural* body, and there is a *spiritual* body. (1 Corinthians 15:34-44)

(please, turn the page)

Wherefore he saith, AWAKE THOU THAT SLEEPEST, *and* ARISE FROM THE DEAD, *and* CHRIST SHALL GIVE THEE LIGHT. See then that ye walk <u>CIRCUMSPECTLY</u>,

**not as <u>FOOLS</u>,**

*but* as WISE,

# <u>R-E-D-E-E-M-I-N-G</u>

# <u>T-H-E</u>   <u>T-I-M-E</u>,

*because*

**the days are EVIL.**

*Wherefore*

**BE YE <u>NOT</u> UNWISE,**

*but*

**UNDERSTANDING WHAT THE WILL OF THE LORD IS.**

(Ephesians 5:14-17)

www.ingramcontent.com/pod-product-compliance
Lightning Source LLC
Chambersburg PA
CBHW061732020426
42331CB00006B/1210